MEXICO'S VOLCANOES

MEXICO'S VOLCANOES

A CLIMBING GUIDE

R.J. Secor

The Mountaineers • Seattle

THE MOUNTAINEERS:
Organized in 1906
" . . . to explore, study, preserve, and enjoy
the natural beauty of the Northwest."

Published by The Mountaineers
715 Pike Street, Seattle, Washington 98101

Published simultaneously in Canada by
Douglas & McIntyre, Ltd.
1615 Venables Street, Vancouver, British Columbia V5L 2H1

Printed in the United States of America

Design by Elizabeth Watson
Maps by Karen Lemagie
Sketches by Dee Molenaar
Cover: Climber on Popocatepetl's Las Cruces route at dawn, with Orizaba
in background. Photo by Herb Kincey.
Title page: Approaching the crater rim of Popocatepetl. Photo by Rich Weber.

Library of Congress Cataloging in Publication Data

Secor, R. J.
  Mexico's volcanoes.

  Bibliography: p.
  Includes index.
  1. Mountaineering—Mexico—Guide-books.
2. Volcanoes—Mexico—Guide-books. 3. Mexico—
Description and travel—1951-   —Guidebooks.
I. Mountaineers (Society) II. Title.
GV 199.44.M6S42   1981   917.2   81-11108
ISBN 0-89886-016-4   AACR2

CONTENTS

Acknowledgments 6
Preface 6
Introduction 7

1. Background 11
   History 11
   Geology 24
   Flora and Fauna 24

2. Preparations 25
   Equipment 25
   Maps 27
   Transportation 28
   Food and Water 29
   Health 32
   Clubs and Guides 35
   Bandits 36
   Climate, Weather, and Snow Conditions 37
   Human Impact 39
   Getting Out of Mexico City 40

3. Popocatepetl and Iztaccihuatl 42
   Climbing Routes on Popocatepetl 48
   Climbing Routes on Iztaccihuatl 66

4. El Pico de Orizaba 82
   Climbing Routes 88

5. Other Volcanoes 102
   Cofre de Perote 103
   La Malinche 104
   Nevado de Toluca 105
   Nevado de Colima 108

Appendices 109
   A. Recommended Reading 109
   B. Speaking Spanish 110
      Pronunciation Guide 110
      Climbing Vocabulary 112
      Climbing Phrases 115
   C. Equipment List 117
   D. Metric Conversions 118

Index 119

ACKNOWLEDGMENTS

Herb Kincey critically reviewed the text and provided photographs.

Zell Rust and Gloria Carlson reviewed and corrected my Spanish. I take full responsibility for any remaining errors.

Otis McAllister provided the bulk of the historical information, and it is regrettable that he passed away before this book came into print.

John Pollock helped get this book started, and Ann Cleeland took on editorial responsibilities; I am very grateful for their tolerance and persistence. Donna DeShazo deserves credit for the fine collection of maps and photographs.

PREFACE

The number of Americans visiting Mexico's volcanoes has increased greatly over the past 10 years. It is my hope that this slim guide will add to the enjoyment of those exploring the alpine regions of Mexico.

There is much more to Mexico than its mountains. Each city, town, and village has a special character of its own, and the foreign visitor who doesn't make the effort to uncover these unique attributes will return with little more than a "peak-bagging" experience. Most Mexicans are friendly, courteous, and willing to offer assistance to the best of their ability; they set an excellent example for other people of the world.

In a similar vein, the foreign visitor should set a good example so that future visitors will be welcome. Tourists must respect the property of others and leave wild areas in their natural state. The climber's concern for the alpine environment of the volcanoes may help encourage other tourists and local residents to leave these great peaks without blight. Let us not allow increased usage of the high volcanoes to lead to environmental costs.

This guidebook is not a substitute for mountaineering skill, experience, or judgment. The tourist routes on these mountains may appear simple, but several insidious dangers are always present on these volcanoes. Inexperienced mountaineers are urged to take advantage of instruction and training provided by various mountaineering clubs before attempting any high mountain ascent.

R. J. Secor
Pasadena, California
June 1981

INTRODUCTION

Two mountain ranges traverse the Mexican republic roughly from north to south. The eastern chain is the Sierra Madre Oriental and is characteristically of low relief and lacking in prominent peaks. The Sierra Madre Occidental serves as the western range and forms a land barrier between the Pacific Ocean and the interior of the country. It averages 3000 m (10,000') in elevation, covers a greater area, and is much more rugged than the Sierra Madre Oriental. It is an arid region and is seldom visited. Aside from a few towns and mines, there are scant means of access. Most of this range has never been mapped authoritatively. The main attractions of this area to the hiker aren't the mountains, peaks, or ridges, but the canyons created by rivers that rush down the western slope into the Pacific and the Gulf of California. Quite often the vertical relief exceeds 1500 m (5000'). A case in point is the Urique River, which cut the Barranca del Cobre southeast of Chihuahua. Parts of this canyon have never been explored, and some believe it is wider and deeper than the Grand Canyon of the Colorado River in Arizona.

Between these two mountain ranges is the Central Plateau of Mexico. The northern part of the plateau is desert, similar to that of eastern New Mexico and western Texas; it is sparsely populated. The southern section has a moist climate, fertile soil, and is thus more heavily populated. Mexico City lies in the valley of Mexico at the extreme southern end of the plateau, and on a clear day two permanently snow-covered volcanoes can be seen to the southeast.

The Mexican volcanoes run approximately along the 19th parallel, a line just south of Mexico City. The westernmost of these peaks is the Nevado de Colima at 4450 m (14,600') above sea level. The range is anchored on the east by El Pico de Orizaba, only 110 km (68.4 mi) from the Gulf of Mexico. These volcanic peaks mark the southern extension of North American physiographic features; some geographers regard this volcanic fracture zone as the southern termination of the North American continent. The range is known variously as the Cordillera de Anahuac, the Sierra Volcanica Transversal, or the Cordillera Neovolcanica.

Most Americans who visit central Mexico for the purpose of hiking and climbing concentrate on the three highest volcanoes—El Pico de Orizaba (5700 m; 18,700'), Popocatepetl (5452 m; 17,887'), and Iztaccihuatl or "Ixta" (5286 m; 17,342'). Altitude is the only major difficulty usually encountered on these mountains. And herein lies the attraction of these mountains: they allow mountaineers to climb to 5000 m (16,400') with a minimum of expense and time from the United States, thus allowing the climber to experience high altitude (though the total amount of time spent above 4300 m or 14,000' is usually less than 24 hours). Equipment needed is the same as would be required for a climb of any of the major Cascade peaks or for a spring climb in the Sierra Nevada of California. Technical difficulties are minimal, though occasionally snow and ice conditions demand the use of an ice axe, crampons, and rope.

7

Most mountaineers who climb Mexico's highest volcanoes climb them by way of their "tourist routes." While I do not belittle these great peaks, nor their "easy" routes (which have, on occasion, claimed the lives of climbers), I will point out their other routes and a few of the other mountains in this area.

This modest volume should not be considered a comprehensive guidebook to this range. Preference has been given to the higher, more prominent volcanoes and their most aesthetic means of ascent. Those interested in hiking up some of the lower volcanoes should contact the Club de Exploraciones de México, which has records on most of the mountains in the country.

The names of Mexico's volcanic mountains seem to be continually in dispute. Many Mexicans prefer to call them by their Aztec names, for example using the name, Citlaltepetl, for the more modern El Pico de Orizaba. Others are in favor of the Spanish names. I prefer to use the Spanish names wherever possible and apologize to those who may be offended by this.

The elevations of these mountains are also disputed. I have seen six different elevations listed for Nevado de Colima, and the height of El Pico de Orizaba varies as much as 500 m (1600') from map to map. This book uses the elevations determined by the Mexican government. Conversions to feet are rounded off.

One of the principal difficulties encountered when visiting these mountains is the approach; sometimes the ascents seem trivial by comparison. Remote roads are often suitable only for trucks and other high-clearance vehicles; dry or wet weather often makes a considerable difference in their condition. Often the roads are unmarked. Please keep these points in mind when searching for a remote roadhead.

There are two unpleasant facets to exploring these mountains; the occasional lack of water and the abundance of litter surrounding the huts, routes, and summits of the higher peaks. The first problem can be taken care of by advance planning. The second is not so easy, for a party should pack out its own garbage, in addition to what is found on the mountain, and this latter amount can be considerable. With the exception of the hut at Tlamacas, none of the other high mountain structures has sanitary facilities. The nearest open window is often used as a garbage chute. Visitors to these mountains would be doing those who follow a considerate service by removing their own rubbish and tidying up the huts as best they can.

Some people who climb these mountains appear to be mere "peak baggers." As soon as they are through with one volcano, they begin their ascent of another. Granted, the objective of most of these parties is to climb peaks, but the trip would undoubtedly be much more pleasant if more time were scheduled between climbs to explore the surrounding area and become acquainted with the people, Aztec ruins, restaurants, markets, and fiestas. Such a change in attitude could turn a "climbing trip" into a "climbing holiday," and considering the relative prices between the United States and Mexico, this prospect becomes quite attractive.

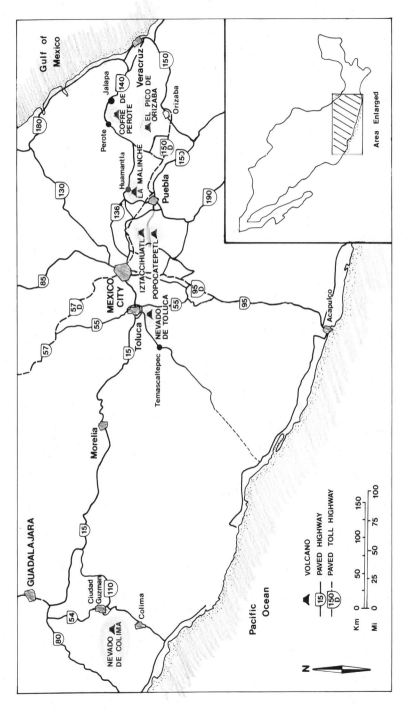

Gulf of Mexico

150

Veracruz

Jalapa ● COFRE DE [140]

Perote ● COFRE DE PEROTE

EL PICO DE ORIZABA

Orizaba

180

130

[150] D

[153]

Huamantla

LA MALINCHE

Puebla

190

136

IZTACCIHUATL

POPOCATEPETL

85

MEXICO CITY

95 D

Acapulco

57 D

55

55

95

57

Toluca

15

NEVADO DE TOLUCA

Temascaltepec

Morelia

GUADALAJARA

15

15

Ciudad Guzman

110

Colima

54

80

NEVADO DE COLIMA

Pacific Ocean

N

Gulf of Mexico

Area Enlarged

▲ VOLCANO

──15── PAVED HIGHWAY

──150 D── PAVED TOLL HIGHWAY

Km 0   50   100   150

Mi 0   25   50   75   100

9

Ovens near Acatzingo (Rich Weber photo)

CHAPTER ONE

BACKGROUND

HISTORY

The Aztecs were one of the most civilized and powerful groups of Indians in the New World. For over 300 years they occupied the Valley of Mexico and surrounding areas, and from the capital city of Tenochtitlán (located near Mexico City), the Aztecs controlled a large empire that included most of central and southern Mexico. In addition to the prominent pyramids, they showed remarkable ingenuity in other areas of engineering. Tenochtitlán was built up from the shallow waters of Lake Texcoco; it was connected to the mainland on the north, west, and south by earthen causeways with movable drawbridges. Aqueducts carried fresh water into the city from springs in the nearby hills. The city had an estimated population of 100,000 when Cortés arrived.

Agriculture formed the basis of the Aztec economy, and although the soil was cultivated by means of simple digging sticks (they had no plows, beasts of burden, or iron tools), the farmers were able to produce enough food to supply not only their own needs, but also those of the workers and government officials in the city.

The Aztecs were famous warriors, with a highly developed military organization. When their armies went to war, they fought not only for political and economic advantage, but also for prisoners who were needed for large-scale human sacrifice. The Aztecs' complex religious practices formed the basis of their culture.

The Aztecs named the surrounding high mountains after their gods and religious legends. Citlaltepetl is Aztec for "The Star Mountain" and this name is connected with the legend that the body of Quetzalcoatl, the Plumed Ser-·pent, was consumed by divine fire in the crater of the volcano. Quetzalcoatl, the Aztec god of learning and the priesthood, then took human form and sailed across the sea, bound to return to the land of the Aztec in the future.

The Aztec name, Popocatepetl, is translated "The Smoking Mountain." According to legend, Popocatepetl, a warrior, was enamored of Iztaccihuatl ("The Sleeping Woman"), daughter of the emperor. When Popocatepetl was returning from a victory in war to claim his beloved, his rivals sent word that he had been killed, and Iztaccihuatl died of grief. Popocatepetl then built the great mountains that lie southeast of Tenochtitlán; on one he placed her body, and on the other he stands holding her funeral torch.

Before the Spanish conquest, Popocatepetl and Iztaccihuatl were worshiped as deities. At festivals of the mountains (called Tepeylhuitl), there were images of Popocatepetl made of amaranth and corn. (Corn was a sacred plant to the Aztecs; reverence for corn is still manifested by Mexicans today.) In one of the great temples of Tenochtitlán, there was a wooden idol of Iztaccihuatl.

There are no records of Aztec ascents of the high mountains, but it is possible that they climbed these peaks. On the northeast ridge of the Ventorrillo of Popocatepetl, there is a small enclosure of blocks and volcanic ash, the highest known structure of its kind in the region. It was probably built by the Aztecs or Toltecs (forerunners of the Aztecs) around 900 A.D. Several potsherds, as well as a broken piece of jade necklace and fragments of obsidian knives, have been found in the area. Similar relics have been found in the vicinity of Tlamacas.

The nature of the Aztec civilization could have allowed the opportunity to explore the upper reaches of the higher volcanoes. Perhaps on occasion a group of soldiers arrived at the summit of Citlaltepetl to scout the area sur-

[Top right] *The crater of Popocatepetl (R.J. Secor photo)*
[Below] *Iztaccihuatl from Amecameca (Ray Smutek photo)*

rounding Veracruz. Or some priests may have examined the crater of Popocatepetl to discover its hidden meanings. Or a young man may have ventured onto the snow and ice of Iztaccihuatl to satisfy his own curiosity.

In 1518 the governor of Cuba became interested in the mainland west of his island, and assigned Hernando Cortés to command the small fleet and army that he was sending to explore and look for treasure. Cortés at first explored and charted the coast of Yucatan, then moved north and landed at the present site of Veracruz on March 4, 1519. Indians along the coast had told him of the great wealth of the Aztecs, and after scuttling all of his ships, he set out in August 1519 with "...fifteen horsemen and three hundred foot [soldiers] as well accoutred for war as my resources and the short space of time would permit" to conquer a nation of six million.[1]

When Cortés and his men arrived in Cholula (near Puebla) in October 1519, Popocatepetl was erupting. The Indians assured him that no mortal being would ever be capable of reaching the summit. To respond to this challenge and to satisfy his curiosity about the "secret of this smoke," Cortés sent Diego de Ordaz with nine Spanish soldiers and several Indians to attempt the ascent.

In a letter sent to Carlos V, King of Spain, dated October 30, 1520, Cortés stated:

Eight leagues from this city of Cholula there are two marvelously high mountains whose summits still at the end of August are covered with snow so that nothing else can be seen of them. From the higher of the two both by day and by night a great volume of smoke comes forth and rises up into the clouds as straight as a staff, with such force that although a very violent wind continuously blows over the mountain range, yet it cannot change the direction of the column. Since I have ever been desirous of sending your Majesty a very particular account of everything that I met with in this land, I was eager to know the secret of this which seemed to me not a little marvelous and accordingly I sent ten men such as were well fitted for the expedition with certain natives to guide them to find out the secret of the smoke, where and how it arose. These men set out and made every effort to climb to the summit but without success on account of the thickness of the snow, the repeated windstorms in which ashes from the volcano were blown in their faces, and also the great severity of the temperature, but they reached very near the top, so near in fact that being there when the smoke began to rush out, they reported it did so with such noise and violence that the whole mountain seemed to fall down: thereupon they descended, bringing a quantity of snow and icicles for us to see, which seemed a novelty indeed, it being so hot everywhere in these parts according to the opin-

----

[1] J. Bayard Morris, translator: *Hernando Cortes; Five Letters 1519-1526* (London: George Routledge & Sons, Ltd. 1928), p. 32.

[Right] *Church at Amecameca; Ixta in background (Rich Weber photo)*

ion of explorers up to now: especially since this land is said to be in the twentieth degree of latitude where great heat is always found... .

Two days after leaving Cholula we climbed the pass between the two mountains which I have already described, from which we could discern the province of Chalco belonging to Moctezuma... .

Early the next day I struck camp for a town two leagues further on called Amecameca, capital of the province of Chalco, which must number more than twenty thousand people, including the villages for some two miles around it. In this town we lodged in some excellent dwellings belonging to the chief ruler of the place.[2]

Historians of the Conquest do not agree with Cortés about whether Diego de Ordaz reached the summit. During Cortés' adventures, Ordaz became a bitter opponent, and in the grand tradition of all great adventurers, Cortés played down some of the exploits of his colleagues so attention would not be diverted from himself. Bernal Diaz, who accompanied Cortés during his conquest of Mexico and recorded everything encountered in great detail, gives credit to Ordaz and two companions for the first ascent. Lopez de Gomara gives similar credit in *Historia General de las Indias* (1552). An English translation of Gomara's work reads:

There is a hill eyght leagues from Chollola, called Popocatepec, which is to say, a hill of smoke, for manye tymes it casteth out smoke and fier. Cortez sente thither tenne Spanyardes, with manye Iniians, to carry their vituall, and to guide them in the way. The ascending was very troublesome, and full of craggie rockes. They approached so nigh the toppe, that they heard such a terrible noyse which proceeded from thence, that they durst not goe unto it, for the ground dyd tremble and shake, and great quantitie of Ashes whyche disturbed the way: but yet two of them who seemed to me the most hardie, and desirous to see strange things, went up to the toppe, because they would not returne with a valueless aunswere, and that they myghte not be accompted cowardes, leaving their fellowes behinde them, proceeded forwards. The Indians sayd, what meane these men: for as yet never mortallman tooke such a journey in hande.

These two valiant fellowes passed through ye desert of Ashes, and at length came under a greate smoke verye thicke, and standing there a while, the darknesse vanished partly away, and then appeared the vulcan and concavetie, which was about halfe a league in compasse, out of the whiche the ayre came rebounding, with a greate noyse, very shrill, and whistling, in short that the whole hil did tremble. It was to be compared unto an oven where glass is made. The smoke and heate was so greate, that they could not abide it, and force were constreyned to returne by the way that they had ascended: but they were not gone farre,

[2]*Ibid*, pp. 61-65.

when the vulcan began to lash out flames of fier, ashes and imbers, yea and at last stones of burning fier: and if they had not chanced to finde a rocke, where under they shadowed themsleves, undoubtedly they had there bin burned.[3]

Gomara goes on to report that in 1540 Popocatepetl erupted again, apparently with much greater force than in 1519. It spread ash, "...fifteen leagues distant, and burned the herbes in their gardens, their fieldes of corne, trees, and clothes that lay a drying."

Many alpine historians still question Ordaz's ascent; it seems doubtful that such a climb could be undertaken with the mountain erupting as it was. (However, in 1914 Lassen Peak in northern California violently erupted; and driven by the same curiosity as Diego de Ordaz and his men, a group of local gentlemen reached the summit to witness lakes of molten rock and pyroclastic bombs.) Moreover, Ordaz and his group had no ice axes or crampons. On the other hand, when a sulfur mining operation was established in the crater of Popocatepetl in the late 19th century, the miners climbed the peak daily utilizing *huaraches* ("sandals") as the avant-garde mountaineering footwear of the day.

In any event, Carlos V, the King of Spain, recognized the achievement of Ordaz as successful and allowed the family of Ordaz to commemorate the adventure by assuming a figure of the burning mountain on the family crest.

After Cortés had finished his business in the vicinity of the volcanoes, he went to Tenochtitlán; after much difficulty (and several retreats and advances), he finally captured the city in 1521. After all this activity, ammunition supplies became low, and a group of five conquistadors were dispatched to the crater of Popocatepetl to obtain sulfur, crucially needed for the manufacture of gunpowder. Although the following story of this mission seems incredible, it has been authenticated by every historian of the day.

Francisco Montaño and four others set out for Popocatepetl amid great acclaim. As they approached the base of the volcano, the crowd of sightseers swelled into the thousands; many built makeshift huts and lean-tos to await the outcome. Indians carried ropes, blankets, and bags to assist the soldiers in their duties. The party bivouacked part way up the volcano by digging a cave in the snow, but sulfur fumes and the cold temperatures forced them out, and they stood there shivering in the dark, the stars being obscured by clouds and smoke. While exercising to keep warm, one of the soldiers fell into a crevasse; fortunately he caught himself on a huge icicle and his companions extracted him after some time.

Shortly after they had resumed their ascent, an eruption shook the mountain, and the party ran for shelter from the falling cannonades. One heated rock landed near them, and they crowded around it and warmed themselves. At this point one soldier was too exhausted to continue, and he

---

[3]Francisco Lopez de Gomara, *The Pleasant Historie of the Conquest of Weast India* (London: Henry Bynneman, 1578), pp. 160-161.

17

remained there for their return. As the rest of the party neared the crater, another explosion took place, this time with no convenient shelter.

Fortunately they remained unscathed, and the apprehensive four arrived at the crater rim. When the fumes, smoke, and steam cleared, they could see seething masses of lava beneath them. Occasionally the earth rumbled beneath their feet. The party cast lots to see which one of them would make the descent into the crater. The lot fell to Montaño, and his companions lowered him into the crater with a rope tied around his waist. The rope was probably a thin cord woven by Indians, perhaps some short ropes tied together. Montaño regarded the rope as an extremely slender support, which might at any moment break and send him into the hell that lay beneath him. Fortunately, the rope held, and Montaño's companions raised and lowered him seven times, each time delivering a bag of sulfur. Juan de Larios then relieved the exhausted Montaño and made six trips into the crater. Montaño later stated that he was lowered into the crater a distance of 200 m (657'), with swimming brain, oppressed by fumes, and in danger of being hit by eruptive substances. As a result of the efforts of the two men, 140 kilograms of sulfur were obtained. Deeming this sufficient, the men started their descent. After threading their way through several crevasses (and falling into a couple), slipping on the icy surfaces, and colliding with sharp projections of loose-lying rocks, they approached their camp at the foot of Popocatepetl. The natives came forth with enthusiastic cheers and took the adventurers on their shoulders. The journey to Coyuhuacan (near Tlaxcala) was a triumphal march, and Cortés himself is said to have welcomed them with an embrace. In Cortés' fourth letter to the king, dated October 15, 1524, he described their sulfur mining operation and added: "...in the future this method of procuring it will be unnecessary; it is certainly dangerous and I am continually writing to Spain to provide us...."[4]

_____

The 19th century saw a reawakening in explorations of the volcanoes. On September 28, 1803, Baron Alexander von Humboldt climbed Nevado de Toluca while examining the vertical distribution of plants and animals. Prior to visiting Mexico he and his companion, Aime Bonpland, climbed to 5878 m (19,286') on Chimborazo in Ecuador. This set a new altitude record for Europeans (the previous record was set by Cortés' soldiers on Popocatepetl). During his year-long stay in Mexico, Humboldt also explored the lower reaches of Cofre de Perote and El Pico de Orizaba, but did not reach their summits. Humboldt's chief concern while in Mexico was a geographic survey of the country, and his busy schedule precluded any other ascents of the high mountains.

In March 1847, 10,000 American soldiers under the command of Major General Winfield Scott landed near Veracruz. Their mission: to take Mexico City and ultimately gain a victory for the United States in the war with Mexico. In six months the troops had conquered the city, but it wasn't until February

_____

[4]Morris, op. cit., p. 275.

1848 that the Treaty of Guadalupe Hidalgo was signed. During this interim period, many American soldiers explored the area surrounding Mexico City, Puebla, and Veracruz, cities they occupied at that time. Undoubtedly they were influenced by the writings of Humboldt, who was becoming popular in the United States during this period. They made numerous excursions to the pyramids of Teotihuacan and Cholula. A party of Americans climbed Popocatepetl; and a group of American soldiers, led by Lt. William F. Reynolds, climbed El Pico de Orizaba during the occupation of Puebla.

Not much is known about Reynolds and his ascent of Orizaba. He was accompanied by a man named Maynard and several soldiers. There appears to be no record of the ascent in any official documents concerning the Mexican War; evidently there was no military rationale for the ascent. It seems to be as difficult to find a logical reason for their ascent as it is to find a logical explanation for the Mexican War! Reynolds' party didn't climb the mountain for purposes of intelligence or signaling; the climb was apparently undertaken for its own sake.

Several residents of Mexico didn't believe that the Reynolds party had reached the summit of Orizaba. In 1851 a group of 40 men set out to climb the peak; and as the journey progressed, several members of the party slowly dropped out from the attempt. At last a lone Frenchman, Alexander Daignon, reached the summit and found a tattered American flag with "1848" carved in the staff.

———————

The first ascent of Iztaccihuatl was the great remaining challenge. Some have given credit to a German named Sonneschmit for the first ascent in 1772; I am inclined to disbelieve this claim, considering the difficulties that parties encountered a hundred years later. Furthermore, if Sonneschmit was successful, then he climbed Iztaccihuatl 14 years before the first ascent of Mont Blanc.

All of the early attempts on Iztaccihuatl were done directly from Amecameca utilizing either Ayoloco or Ayolotepito glaciers, located on the western side of the mountain. During the late 1850s a geographic and geological survey was conducted in the vicinity of Iztaccihuatl and Popocatepetl, and there were two or three attempts to reach the top of Iztaccihuatl. The principal character behind these endeavors was Walker Fearn, the Secretary of the United States Legation in Mexico. Invariably these ascents were unsuccessful due to icy conditions and the lack of crampons and proper ice axes.

Years later a Briton attempted the peak without "rope or ice axe" for his Indian guide assured him that they were unnecessary. Upon arrival at the snout of the glacier the guide, "...urged an immediate return, confessing that he had never gone further himself, and that he believed the mountain to be inaccessible." But they continued and "My guide (?), who followed me at a distance of about twenty yards, evidently thought the whole proceeding to be a good example of Englishman's idiocy." Unfortunately, "...we found it impossible to proceed without danger and were reluctantly compelled to return, as a steep ice-slope about fifty yards wide effectively barred further progress to anyone unaided by an ice axe."[5]

In November of 1889, H. Remsen Whitehouse took time off from his diplomatic duties while serving as the British Minister to Mexico and set out for Iztaccihuatl. He was accompanied by Baron von Zedwitz, the German Minister to Mexico. In two days they established themselves in a cave near the terminus of the Ayoloco Glacier on the western side of the mountain. At four o'clock the next morning, they started up the glacier. Bare ice in the icefall presented some difficulty, but they made quick work of it by cutting steps with the wood axe they had brought along for such a situation. At nine o'clock that morning they arrived at the summit, only to discover a bottle with a calling card inside. James de Salis, a Swiss mountaineer who had attempted Iztaccihuatl for over a period of two years had reached the summit five days before Whitehouse and von Zedwitz.

In 1917 a recent graduate of Harvard University—Otis McAllister— started work with the Southern Pacific Railroad, which was involved with construction and maintenance of railways in Mexico. He was based in the Yaqui Indian region of northern Mexico, at Emplane, Sonora; and he spent his free time climbing many of the neighboring hills by himself. He had already had considerable mountaineering experience. Before attending Harvard, McAllister had made several explorations in the West—in the hills surrounding San Francisco and the mountains around Lake Tahoe. He joined one of the first Sierra Club outings to the Sierra Nevada in 1904, and had the privilege of meeting John Muir in the incomparable setting of Yosemite Valley. While attending Harvard, he visited Mount Mitchell in North Carolina and Mount Monadnock in New Hampshire. Over summer holiday he visited Europe and climbed the Piz Languard, the Faulhorn, the Rigi, and the Goerner Grat in the Alps. While in Scotland he climbed Ben Lomond, explored the Lake District of England, and visited Italy where he climbed Vesuvius. Before arriving in Mexico, McAllister climbed Mount Shasta and Mount Whitney in California.

After some time, McAllister was transferred to Mazatlan, but he eventually quit the railroad and moved to Mexico City where he became a schoolteacher. Transportation was difficult in Mexico in the early 1920s, but McAllister managed to visit several of the mountains within the Distrito Federal. He began writing about his trips for a Mexico City newspaper, and gradually his students and other friends began to join him on these outings. In the grand tradition of other great mountaineering clubs, the Club de Exploraciones de México, A.C. (CEMAC)[6] was founded on the summit of Ajusco on March 26, 1922.

---

[5]A.R. Hamilton, "Ascents in Mexico," *The Alpine Journal*, Vol. XVIII (1896-1897), pp. 457-458.

[6]The "A.C." stands for Asociación Civil (civil association), which identifies the group as a non-profit organization.

[Right] *Popo from Paso de Cortés (Rich Weber photo)*

McAllister was the founder of the Club and was its driving force for over 50 years. Its organization was based on that of the Sierra Club, which was founded in San Francisco when McAllister, "…was a tiny chap of three years of age." The Club's emblem has the same fundamental symbolism as the Sierra Club's emblem: the mountain, the tree, and the stream of water. Instead of Half Dome, the great Sequoia, and the Merced River, the Aztec symbols for the mountain, the tree, and the stream are used.

A review of the Club's journal, La Montaña ("The Mountain"), which began publication in 1929, shows that the activities of the group have been similar to those of corresponding U.S. and Canadian clubs. In the early 1920s the Club made ascents of the highest volcanoes and explored the valleys and Aztec ruins surrounding Mexico City. A change of emphasis occurred in the latter part of the decade, when parties began seeking out more difficult routes on the high volcanoes, and technical climbing gained more interest than snow-slogs. In 1929 a party of 12 climbed La Amacuilecatl ("the feet" of Ixta), and another party explored the northern side of La Cabellera ("the hair"). The early part of the next decade saw a traverse of Iztaccihuatl, ascents of the Ventorrillo of Popocatepetl and Las Torrecillas ("Little Towers") on El Pico de Orizaba, and a descent into the crater of Popocatepetl. This last outing was significant in that it eventually led to the formation of a rock climbing group for CEMAC.

In the latter part of the 1930s, the first fatalities occurred to Club members in mountaineering accidents. Issac Valvovinos died in a fall into a crevasse on Iztaccihuatl, and Luis Camacho and Adolfo Esparza met with tragedy on Popocatepetl. Today, the CEMAC schedule carries warnings about these particular routes.

In 1940, Roberto Mangas, who also founded the rock climbing group, became the first to climb the highest mountains in Mexico over 100 times. Later in the same year, he assisted Juan Peimbert in leading 116 climbers on Iztaccihuatl, of which 115 made the summit!

After World War II, numerous special activity groups within CEMAC were formed, including the high mountain, explorations, speleology, rivers, and tourism groups. In 1948, six Club members participated in their first foreign expedition, climbing Aconcagua in Argentina as well as two mountains in Chile. In 1952, two CEMAC members were involved in a Mexican Cruz Roja ("Red Cross") expedition that climbed Mount McKinley in Alaska. The six-member party made the eighth ascent of McKinley; it was the first ascent by a party from outside the United States. The ascent took 13 days from Wonder Lake to the South Summit, by way of the Muldrow Glacier. The Mexicans did not use horses, dog-sleds, or an airplane to help them with the approach; and they did not even have snowshoes for use on the glaciers! The Swiss Foundation for Alpine Research described their ascent as a "tour de force."

While these foreign expeditions were being organized and carried out, Club members put new routes on the north side of "the head" of Iztaccihuatl, the Ventorrillo on Popocatepetl, and on the northwest flank of Orizaba. Simultaneously, Club chapters were being established in such diverse cities as Acapulco and Monterrey. Today, aside from the chapter in Mexico City, there are chapters in 10 other cities in Mexico.

In the 1960s members began making explorations to the farthest mountains within the Republic of Mexico. Numerous canyons were also explored, including the Barranca del Cobre in the Sierra Madre Occidental. It was not until 1968 that a CEMAC party climbed Cerro de la Encantada in Baja California, an important mountain to desert "peak-baggers" from southern California. A member of that first Club trip to Baja, Alfredo Careaga, described this climb as, "A tremendous excursion that tests all of the talents of the mountaineer."

During this time river touring gained more interest, and in 1970 a CEMAC party descended the Cañon del Sumidero in the state of Chiapas, utilizing a variety of techniques. A more ambitious journey was undertaken in 1971, with a party exploring the Amazon River in Brazil.

Also in 1971, several Club members traveled to Yosemite where Juan Gabriel Nieto and Pedro Diaz climbed the Triple Direct on El Capitan. A short time later, the Club de Exploraciones de México, A.C. celebrated its 50th anniversary on March 26, 1972. CEMAC has over 800 members, but for this celebration approximately 2000 people were present. Many of the participants were from associated clubs in Mexico, but there were also several government officials, celebrities, prominent citizens, and foreign diplomats present. Otis McAllister, on behalf of the Club, received a diploma from the President of Mexico, Luis Echeverria, who cited the outstanding contributions the organization had made to the country. McAllister was named Honorary President and Founder of the Club. Everyone saluted each other on their glorious past and set the date for their centennial anniversary, March 26, 2022.

The Club had good cause for celebrating its accomplishments. It has managed to acquire its own building and bus without government, Catholic, or YMCA assistance or influence. The Club is held in high esteem by fellow Mexicans. Seldom have I seen a mountaineering club that can match their enthusiasm.

It seems a pity that North American alpine historians have ignored the sport south of the border. In 1935 the rock climbing group was making class 5 ascents (in the late 1950s, a teenage girl was leading at this level), and the high mountain group was seeking out more difficult routes on the high volcanoes. Considering the support that was then available, it must have taken a good deal of nerve to venture onto "the head" of Iztaccihuatl or the Abanico ("Palisade") of the Ventorrillo on Popocatepetl.

With the increased popularity of climbing in the States and in Europe, more information is arriving in Mexico concerning new developments in mountaineering gear and methods. Fernando Mancilla wrote in the March 1974 *La Montaña*: "Foreign summits will become more accessible, it will be easier to have direct contact with the techniques and equipment from other areas of the world. The Alps, the Andes and the Himalaya are waiting for us."

GEOLOGY

Volcanic activity in central Mexico began approximately 10 million years ago, during the late Miocene and Pliocene epochs. The volcanoes that were formed at that time were the forerunners of those that exist today. During that time Iztaccihuatl was created, and the first of Popocatepetl's cones appeared, the remnant today being the Ventorrillo. Also during that period, the continents had begun to take their present shape, and ancient relatives of humans first appeared.

The next major cycle of volcanic activity began early in the Pleistocene epoch, approximately 2.5 million years ago. The sites of activity generally moved south, and during this period the present cones of Iztaccihuatl, Popocatepetl, and El Pico de Orizaba were formed. Evidence seems to indicate that these original mountains were higher than they are today. Volcanic activity in the early Pleistocene epoch prevented permanent glaciers from forming on the high volcanoes, especially on Popocatepetl. By the end of the Illinoian glacial period, eruptions diminished to allow erosion to do its work, and ice fields developed and still remain on the mountains.

Since this period there have been numerous eruptions, especially on Popocatepetl, and with the exception of Paricutin, these eruptions have not changed the fundamental structure of the mountains. Today all of the volcanoes are dormant, with Popocatepetl spewing steam occasionally.

FLORA AND FAUNA

The vegetation of the Mexican volcanoes varies with the climate, soil, geologic history, and use of land. A common perception of Mexico is one of an arid countryside, with cactus and Joshua trees dotting the landscape. To a certain extent this is correct, but the higher elevations of the volcanoes provide the visitor with dense pine forests and meadows of bunch grass and lupine. In Mexico, the boreal forest is confined to the higher volcanoes, occurring at 2900 to 3600 m (9500' to 11,800'). This is similar to the high mountain forest found in the western United States. This zone is primarily open pine stands (*Pinus montezumae* and its varieties), with an undergrowth of grasses.

A few hardy animals live on the volcanoes. During the evening hours, coyotes roam over the grass; and on a rare occasion, a wolf may be seen. Field mice maintain a hardy existence up to 4200 m (13,800'). Lizards are abundant; on sunny days they can be seen sitting on warm rocks. They have been spotted as high as 4250 m (13,950'). Ravens are often seen flying overhead. It has been rumored that wild dogs, cougars, and jaguars roam the forested slopes of the volcanoes.

Popocatepetl from Amecameca (Rich Weber photo)

CHAPTER TWO

PREPARATIONS

EQUIPMENT

Some prefer to travel light, cutting their toothbrush in half and throwing out books like this one in the quest for ease of mobility. Others prefer to carry the whole catastrophe. But while packing for your trip, keep the following points in mind.

Generally speaking, take along the same equipment as you would carry for a climb of a glaciated Cascade peak or for a spring climb in the Sierra Nevada of California. This includes an ice axe, good boots, crampons, gaiters, wool trousers and sweaters, wind pants, and a wind breaker. Weather conditions can be either hot or cold, so mittens, a down jacket or vest, long underwear, a wool cap, and a scarf are desirable in addition to dark glasses, broad-brimmed hat, and sun screen to protect the climber from high altitude glare, which can be severe. It is smart to bring along a rain jacket and the rain fly for the tent. A sleeping bag that is comfortable below freezing temperatures is necessary. Crevasses are prevalent on the volcanoes, and smart climbers will carry prusik slings, a rope, carabiners, and some type of snow anchors. It is assumed that visiting climbers know how to use all of this stuff.

Most Mexicans leave for the summit at four o'clock in the morning (regardless of the high camp), so a head lamp would be a nice thing to carry. The interiors of the mountain huts are dark, and an ample supply of candles would be handy. There aren't any mattresses in the high mountain huts, so bring your own. On my last trip to the volcanoes, I purchased a 12 liter plastic jug from a local *ferreteria* ("hardware store"). It was used to carry water from the spring to the hut on Orizaba and to hold a temporary supply of gasoline. Then we gave it to a mechanic who had helped us. It cost less than a dollar, and our group unanimously decided to add the item to our list of essentials for a successful climbing trip to Mexico.

Most Americans use white gas or butane stoves for backpacking. Unfortunately, it is next to impossible to locate these fuels in Mexico. I was once told that tailors and dry cleaners sell white gas, but I have found them to be reluctant to part with their limited supply. After inquiring at some Mexico City sporting goods stores, I was told to try a gas station. The gas station sold me unleaded automobile fuel (it is interesting to note that my white gas backpacking stove has run perfectly on this fuel). I have had no luck at all locating a supply of butane cartridges.

To avoid these difficulties, many people bring a supply of fuel with them from the United States. Considering that one cup of gasoline equals the explosive force of 13 sticks of dynamite, it is easy to see why the airlines frown on this type of baggage.

Kerosene is available from most PEMEX stations, and this would appear to be the best type of stove to bring to Mexico. The fuel is inexpensive, widely available, safer, and more efficient than gasoline. The one drawback is that kerosene stoves must be primed with alcohol or gasoline, but the advantages outweigh this inconvenience. It should be mentioned that you will have to provide your own container when purchasing *petroleo* ("kerosene").

I hold a tent to be a grand nuisance while carrying it and an indispensable item once it is set up in the rain and snow. There are huts on all of the popular routes on the high volcanoes, and with good timing, you will have little use for a tent. On weekends and during Christmas holidays, expect to find the huts full, so a tent would fall under the category of "essentials." At other times it is a heavy luxury.

Skis have been used occasionally on the volcanoes, and some think that a pair of ski poles have more utility than an ice axe on the 30° slopes of Popo, Ixta, and Orizaba. Before ski mountaineers start carrying their gear, they should remember how much effort is required to carry skis to an elevation of 5400 to 5700 m (17,700' to 18,700'). Remember, high altitude affects judgment, and it is a long way to the bottom. Once when I was descending Popocatepetl, I saw a gentleman who must have decided that it would be easier to glissade. After a few seconds he realized the error in his judgment, but it was too late. The involuntary glissade was 700 m (2297') long, and he got off lightly with a broken leg, fractured ankle, and numerous other scars and contusions. (While this is not a skiing accident, I believe this incident demonstrates one of the central dangers of these mountains.) Alpine ski touring equipment is the only way to go; the terrain above snow line is not suited for Nordic cross-country gear. But if you are an expert ski mountaineer, the effort should be worth the downhill run.

Other items that come in handy when speaking with locals and making friends are post cards of your hometown (especially buildings and other urban sights) and photographs of your family. Pins and emblems of different mountaineering clubs also are traded extensively. Finally, if you don't enjoy Mexico as it is, please don't go. If you do go, take a lot of friendship. Leave behind the "ugly American" traits of arrogance and self-proclaimed superiority.

MAPS

Mexico is currently in the process of mapping the entire country with maps of 1:50,000 scale. The quality of these maps is equal to the topographic maps put out by the United States Geological Survey; however, some errors are apparent on a few sheets. These maps are relatively expensive, but worth buying. Apparently if maps are ordered from the United States, the price is twice as high.

All of the volcanoes are covered by these sheets, except El Pico de Orizaba (which should be out soon). I would recommend purchasing the maps in Mexico City, to make sure the proper map is received. However, maps can be ordered by mail from DETENAL (formerly CETENAL), San Antonio Abad 124, Mexico 8, D.F. (telephone: 578-62-00, extension 146). A catalog of topographic maps can be obtained from the same address. Response is slow, however; allow four months. When ordering maps, ask for cartas topograficas ("topographic maps"), mentioning the scale and the catalog number. All orders must be accompanied by a cashier's check drawn from a Mexican or U.S. bank, payable in pesos. Checks payable in U.S. dollars will not be accepted.

There are two DETENAL map outlets in Mexico City. One is located at the above address, which can be reached easily by taking Metro Line 2 toward Tasquena and getting off at the San Antonio Abad station. The map outlet is right next to the station. The other outlet is located in downtown Mexico City at Balderas 71. From the airport, take Metro Line 1 and get off at the Balderas station; the office is a short walk to the north.

It is easier to purchase road maps of Mexico in the United States than in

Mexico. American Automobile Association maps are free to members, and many American oil companies provide them for a nominal fee. Often, Mexican insurance companies give away maps and road logs; be sure to ask for them.

TRANSPORTATION

Tourism is one of the leading businesses in Mexico, and it is relatively easy to reach Mexico City from the United States, either by plane, train, bus, or private automobile. Specific information on each of these methods is readily available elsewhere, and since it seems to change everyday, I won't mention it here. Many who visit the volcanoes fly to Mexico City and then rent an automobile to approach the mountains. Renting a car has the advantage of flexibility; the only schedule to meet is your own. The disadvantage is the cost, for flying to Mexico City and then renting an automobile is the most expensive way to visit the volcanoes. But for those who have a limited amount of time, this is the way to go.

For those with a bit more time to spare, the trains that run to Mexico City offer the best bargain of all. These modern passenger trains, which take between 36 and 48 hours from the border to Mexico City, are relatively inexpensive.

Some take the bus to Mexico City, and many utilize this service in getting around from volcano to volcano. The fares are slightly cheaper than those for the trains, but the conditions are somewhat more austere and dangerous. (Those selecting this method of transportation will find the mountains safer than the bus.) All the trips in this book have been done from Mexico City using public transportation. Mexico has an excellent bus system that reaches almost any town that has a road leading to it. As far as coverage and frequency of service are concerned, the system has my highest praise; I just wish the drivers wouldn't pass on blind curves or play "chicken" on those narrow bridges at night (especially when their headlights put out less light than a firefly).

Some drive their own vehicles to central Mexico. The trip takes about three days from the border and has the advantage of being flexible and providing a convenient place to store extra food and equipment while exploring the mountains. It may also be easier to visit the trailheads. However, most American insurance policies are not honored south of the border. A Mexican auto insurance policy is not required to drive in Mexico, but is highly recommended; if you are in an accident without insurance, you will most likely go to jail for quite a long time. A policy can be purchased easily in most border towns.

Whether you drive your own car to Mexico or rent one upon arrival, the following points on driving in the country may be useful. I don't drive at night in Mexico, and I don't recommend it. The roads are often in fair to poor shape, and cattle frequently wander onto the roads at night because the

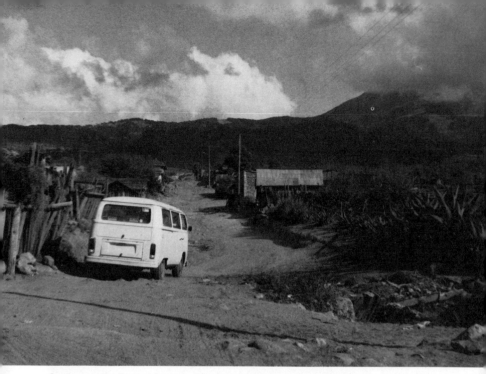

On the road to Piedra Grande (R.J. Secor photo)

pavement is warmer than the fields. (Many buses have "cattle-catchers" built into their front grills.) Sometimes drivers will signal that it is safe to pass by blinking their left turn signal. This is unnerving when done on blind curves and hills or, after having taken advantage of the advice, having the driver suddenly turn left onto some obscure side road. Often bridges have room for only one vehicle at a time; right of way is given to the driver who flashes the headlights first. I always let the other driver go first.

On the *carreterras* ("highways") most of these hazards are absent, but it should be noted that these toll roads are expensive; the tolls almost equal the cost of gasoline for the stretch covered. I have often found that the *libre* ("free") roads, which run more or less parallel to the turnpikes, are just as fast and more scenic and interesting than their nearest competition.

FOOD AND WATER

When I travel to Mexico, I usually purchase most of my food upon arrival. This makes my luggage lighter and I save a little money, for most of the goods are cheaper south of the border. *Supermercados* ("supermarkets") carry the same fare as their counterparts in the United States. However, it is difficult to locate the smaller sizes of canned meat, vegetables, and other products; most of these goods seem to come in the larger "economy" sizes.

In the market, Amecameca (Rich Weber photos)

Instant hot breakfasts and powdered soups don't seem to be available, so come prepared.

Many people from the United States who set out to climb the high volcanoes abstain from Mexican food in any way, shape, or form. This is regrettable, for one of the joys of visiting other areas is sampling the local foods, and I would encourage anyone visiting Mexico to try the offerings. To avoid illness, I follow this general rule: I don't put anything into my mouth that is questionable (and the local water is always questionable). First-class restaurants (usually found in tourist hotels) are reasonably safe, but with this security comes a price. The only general advice I can give is to look the restaurant over. If you would feel comfortable eating food that comes from the kitchen, then have your meal there. It is a good idea to eat only those fruits and vegetables that can be peeled.

Don't drink the water south of the border; if you touch the wrong stuff, it can put you on your ear for a long time. If you're in a restaurant and ask for *agua purificado* ("pure water"), the waiter will probably bring you water from the tap, so it's better to drink beverages that don't have water or even ice cubes in them. I have gotten sick only once while in Mexico; I believe that this was due to brushing my teeth with tap water. I had *"turista"* (diarrhea) for two days, and after that I never got sick again, mainly due to paranoia.

The best time of the year to visit central Mexico is during the winter "dry" season, November through March. This lack of rain and snow makes the climbing and hiking easier, but it tends to dry up the high mountain streams. To add to the problem, volcanic rock and soil do an excellent job of absorbing water. Under these conditions, the possibility of locating a running stream above timber line is remote. Of the few streams that are running, remember that none of the huts have sanitary facilities, and most garbage is deposited through the nearest open (or broken) window. It is usually best to carry an alternative supply of water.

I would recommend purchasing bottled water in one of the larger cities, such as Mexico City or Puebla. Many of the smaller towns aren't stocked with it (an exception is Amecameca). You will have to provide your own container or pay a deposit on a *garrafon*, a 20 liter (5 gallon) glass bottle. It might be better to purchase some plastic jugs from a hardware store, put the water in these, and then label them in *both* English and Spanish *petroleo* ("kerosene"), *gasolina* ("gasoline") or perhaps a Mr. Yuk or a skull and crossbones. No one ever steals water with these labels.

At one time the party I was with ran short of water and was unable to locate a supply of *agua purificado*. We had only enough water for cooking, not enough to climb the mountain. What to do? We stocked up on beer, soft drinks, and fruit juices; and I can honestly say that our climb of Orizaba was fueled by Cerveza Tecate, a local brew.

HEALTH

I know as much about medicine as most politicians know about their constituents. But visitors may want to keep the following points in mind.

Water found below timber line is always suspect. The most effective treatment of questionable water is boiling for 20 minutes. As far as chemical treatment is concerned, iodine appears to be more effective than chlorine. Even many Mexicans are not immune to the effects of their own water; immunity occurs as one's body gains resistance to the germs found in the local water and food, a process that can take a long time.

Lomotil, a drug that many people take for diarrhea, is available over-the-counter at *farmacias* ("pharmacies") in Mexico. However, it may be better to let the diarrhea run its course rather than hinder it. If the diarrhea doesn't clear up in a few days, go to a physician and make sure you don't have dysentery or hepatitis.

No shots are required for entry into Mexico, but many doctors recommend a gamma globulin shot to protect against hepatitis. I was amazed at my companions during my last trip to the volcanoes. I had never seen a group of people more cautious about the local food. Yet none of them had taken the precaution of obtaining a gamma globulin injection before leaving the States.

People have different reactions when exposed to altitude, and I seem to react differently each time I go above 4600 m (15,110′). This is undoubtedly due to several intervening variables for both myself and other people. Researchers have spent a considerable amount of time studying altitude illness, but thus far, there have been few significant results. A noted authority on the subject, Dr. Charles S. Houston, has stated, "At present we have no way of predicting who will and who will not have altitude sickness."[1]

Because most climbers on the Mexican volcanoes tend to gain a lot of altitude fast, they should be prime candidates for mountain sickness, including high altitude pulmonary edema, cerebral edema, and retinal hemorrhages. Several incidents of these illnesses have been reported in recent years. Shortly after Hernando Manzanos made the first technical ascent of the Cabellera of Iztaccihuatl in the mid-1950s, he became ill and eventually died. The illness was diagnosed as "acute pneumonia," but current evidence seems to indicate that it was actually pulmonary edema.

The risk of pulmonary edema and cerebral edema increases with too rapid an ascent at over 3000 m (10,000′). The recommended rate of ascent over 3000 m is 300 m (1000′) per day. One authority has recommended spending two nights in Mexico City (2100 m; 7000′), one night at 3000 m (10,000′), one night at 3870 m (12,700′), and another night at 4900 m (16,000′) before attempting a summit.[2] However, these are impractical rates on the Mexican volcanoes. It would appear that the mountaineer's dictum, "Climb high, sleep low," is the best method of preventing mountain sickness, and this method is widely practiced by mountaineers in Mexico.

Acute Mountain Sickness occurs after too rapid an ascent to 1500-1800 m (5000-6000′). Symptoms include headache, dizziness, drowsiness, shortness of breath, nausea, and sometimes vomiting. The best cure is rest and descent to a lower elevation. At a lower altitude, the sickness usually subsides fairly quickly.

High Altitude Pulmonary Edema is much more serious, comes on rapidly, and has been known to cause death less than 40 hours after a rapid climb to 3000 m (10,000′). The symptoms include a cough with bloody or foamy sputum, shortness of breath, general weakness, and a gurgling sound in the chest. If any of these symptoms appear, assume the worst and get the victim

---

[1]Charles S. Houston, M.D., "Altitude Illness—Recent Advances in Knowledge," *The American Alpine Journal*, Vol. 22, No. 1 (1979), p. 155.

[2]*Mountain Safety Research Newsletter*, No. 11 (Mar. 1976), p. 10.

to a lower elevation as soon as possible. Dr. Houston notes, "High altitude pulmonary edema may proceed rapidly to coma and death, or may improve with equal speed if the victim goes down only a few thousand feet after symptoms begin."[3] If oxygen is available, it would be advisable to administer it (some better *farmacias* in Mexico City sell small canisters of oxygen).

Cerebral Edema is not common but is the most serious of the three. Symptoms include a severe headache, staggering, and hallucinations, which could lead to coma and death. It rarely occurs below 4200 m (13,780′).

Those going above timber line should be aware of hypothermia and prepare accordingly. Whether you are the type who can't differentiate between a butterfly closure and a Band-Aid, or one of those who has the capability of performing an apendectomy standing in slings on the Big Wall, you should carry an adequate first aid kit, with knowledge of how to use the contents.

Fortunately, the three major volcanoes have facilities for registration of climbs; and if your party doesn't return at the appointed hour, people will be worried about you. For that matter, if you leave on a climb and don't register, the personnel manning these stations will possibly be offended. It is always a good idea to register in advance and to sign out upon return. For Popocatepetl and Iztaccihuatl, register at the Vincente Guerrero Lodge; on weekends the Socorro Alpino de México ("Mountain Rescue Group of Mexico") is in attendance and gives free advice. Donations are actively solicited. Give generously; remember Karma! For El Pico de Orizaba, register with Señor Reyes at La Antigua Flor in Tlachichuca. He has a climbing register that goes back many years, and visitors should not miss the opportunity to add their names to this historic document.

In the event of an accident on Popocatepetl or Iztaccihuatl, notify the Socorro Alpino de México at the Vincente Guerrero Lodge at Tlamacas or the Cruz Roja at Amecameca. On El Pico de Orizaba, contact Señor Reyes at La Antigua Flor in Tlachichuca; since he owns the only telephone in town, he is in a much better position to notify the Cruz Roja than anyone else. For the other mountains, contact the Cruz Roja or El Seguro Social (Social Security) for assistance. This latter organization is Mexico's national health service; most towns have such clinics. Fortunately their locations are marked on the topographic maps issued by the government. Look for the black dots with the white crosses.

Try to leave someone with the injured climber. Try to send at least two people for help. Complete information is needed: How many are injured? Extent of injuries? Manpower on the scene? The exact location? Equipment available? Equipment and manpower needed? (The Mexican military has high altitude helicopters, but don't count on their availability.) Don't expect

---

[3]Houston, *op. cit.*, p. 154.

anyone to speak English, so preferably one of the messengers should have a working command of Spanish or at least a dictionary.

The Mexican rescue groups are dependable and extremely skilled (they make up for their poor equipment with their climbing ability). But help may be a long time in coming. Delays from 24 to 72 hours are common. Hopefully, all parties climbing the volcanoes will be self-sufficient in the event of an accident. When time is of the essence, the resources of your own party can make all the difference.

CLUBS AND GUIDES

Considerable discussion has been given to this facet of mountaineering in Mexico in the history section of this book. Those in search of more up-to-date information on the volcanoes can contact the Club de Exploraciones de México at Apartado Postal 10134, Mexico 8, D.F. Their clubhouse is located at Juan A. Mateos 146 in the same postal zone; the phone number is 578-57-30. Meetings are held every night of the week; on Wednesday nights there is usually a program presented at nine o'clock. English conversation is available at 7:00 P.M. Wednesdays and Fridays. If you are planning a trip to Mexico, whether it is car camping, backpacking, or climbing, you can contact the Club about information on the specific area you are planning to visit. You may also want to send for a copy of their schedule of programs and trips. Non-members are not always welcome on some of their outings, unless they are the guests of a member in good standing. But their programs are open to everyone, and foreign visitors are treated as special guests.

There are several other mountaineering clubs in Mexico. The Club Citlaltepetl is based in Puebla and serves as the primary authority on El Pico de Orizaba. The Seccion Alta Montaña of the Cruz Roja and the Socorro Alpino de México specialize in mountain rescue, and their members have made ascents of some of the great mountains of the world. In 1952 the Cruz Roja organized and carried out an ascent of Mount McKinley, and in recent years some members of the Socorro Alpino de México have visited the Himalaya. El Grupo de los Cien ("the Group of One Hundred") constructed most of the mountain huts on the volcanoes during the 1950s. Dios y Montaña consists of members of the clergy and laymen who actively visit the mountains; they are chiefly responsible for the numerous crosses, memorials, and shrines, which can be seen on the prominent routes of the volcanoes. Youth groups, churches, and boy scouts also make up a sizable portion of the Mexican mountaineering community.

Arrangements can be made for guides through these clubs. But be forewarned: this can be expensive. The client is responsible for food, transportation, and other expenses for the guide, in addition to his normal fee. Often, the guide will require an unusual diet, and can incur numerous other expenses. If you need a guide, attempt to make agreements concerning the fee in advance of the trip. However, if you are interested in just the standard

Señor Reyes' store, La Antigua Flor, Tlachichuca (R.J. Secor photo)

routes of the volcanoes or are interested in hiking with no particular objective, a guide will probably be an unnecessary expense.

In some towns and villages, pack animals with driver can be rented. The animals may be horses, mules, or burros and may or may not come with saddles and pack frames. Such luxuries may seem unnecessary, but with bargaining, the price can be brought down low enough to make it very attractive. There are no set fees or practices; each driver seems to have his own customs and ways of doing business. I have never taken advantage of such a service, but friends have reported rates that have been inexpensive. For some of the remote approaches to El Pico de Orizaba or for remote mountains and canyons, this may be an attractive way to travel.

BANDITS

I have never encountered a bandit in Mexico. But this appears to be the number one fear of Americans visiting Mexico. The Club de Exploraciones de México has the following rules "...to maintain the security of the group": *Have no less than four people in the group. The group stays together, no exceptions. Carry your camera in your knapsack, and take it out only when you are using it. Avoid attracting attention to yourself or to the group. And no alcoholic beverages or firearms are allowed.* This advice must be sound, for CEMAC has not experienced a holdup since 1932.

It may be comforting for uneasy people to note that most of the "professional thieves" (this includes mercenaries, kidnappers, pickpockets, assassins, bank robbers, and international jewel thieves) hang out in the big cities of Mexico and in the resort towns. But there is still the possibility that the "amateurs" (this includes the local population *and* foreigners) will stroll by your hut or campsite and help themselves to whatever goodies happen to be lying around.

I am more afraid of the police than I am of bandits. I know that those men in uniform can make things far worse for an unsuspecting *gringo* than any modern day *bandito.* Don't argue with the police. Keep a cool head, relax, offer them candy or cigarettes during the conversation. Remember, the police are in charge, and you are their subjects.

Avoid wearing clothing or using equipment that can be even remotely associated with the military. Someone spotting a man wearing fatigues, a khaki shirt, and a beret will conclude that guerillas are in the vicinity. I once took a green duffel bag with me to Mexico. While driving in Mexico City early one morning, an astute policeman spotted the olive drab color in the back of my car. Soon I was in the middle of 4 police cars and 10 policemen. After 20 minutes, everything was straightened out, but they gave me a good lecture that impressed upon me how foolish I had been.

The best advice to avoid trouble is: Don't do anything stupid. Carrying a camera into a crowded market is stupid. Leaving your possessions unattended, even for a second, is stupid. Camping near a populated area without a guard is stupid. Attracting attention to yourself (by appearance or actions) is stupid. Making enemies instead of friends is stupid. Think about the security of your own party and those who might follow. And don't do anything stupid!

Don't be overly concerned about getting ripped off. It is an excellent way to spoil a good trip. Just be cautious, and remember that in the countryside, most of these human dangers are absent, and it is a relatively safe place to be.

CLIMATE, WEATHER, AND SNOW CONDITIONS

The rainy season in Mexico is during the summer months, and this makes hikes and climbs in the mountains unpleasant and to a certain extent, hazardous. Avalanches have been known to occur during this period of wet weather and warm temperatures. White-outs are also prevalent, along with thunderstorms. The volcanoes can be climbed year-round, but the odds for success lie in the dry winter, the period from November to March. All of the above-mentioned conditions can also occur during this period, but their frequency is at a much lower level. Anyone headed above the snowline should be prepared for the possibility of storms, white-outs, and icy snow conditions.

Lenticular cloud caps can be seen over the volcanoes on occasion, and the prudent mountaineer will take compass bearings on prominent landmarks to ensure a quick and safe return. The mean freezing level is at 4200 m (approximately 14,000'). Timber line is at 4000 m (13,000').

I saw Popocatepetl covered with 30 centimeters of powder snow one year, and another year it was a continuous sheet of ice. These conditions vary with the amount of precipitation versus sunshine, freeze-thaw, and the general weather for the given year. The southern sides of the higher peaks are often completely bare of snow, and this makes travel unpleasant at higher elevations. Popo, Ixta, and Orizaba are the only peaks in Mexico with permanent snow.

When is the best time to visit the volcanoes? Weather and climatic factors aside, it appears that Christmas is the most popular time for people north of the border to visit the mountains. This gives the opportunity to speak with mountaineers from all over the United States and Canada, and many foreign countries as well. The disadvantage of this time is that the huts may be full.

HUMAN IMPACT

If you haven't figured it out yet, these mountains see a lot of traffic. This should come as no surprise, for one of the world's largest cities is nearby and the number of foreign visitors is increasing every year. Mexico's bureaucracy has not yet reached such an advanced state where the number of climbers is controlled by a quota system. Visitors can help maintain the aesthetic beauty of these mountains by following a few suggestions.

When camping below 4000 m (13,000'), be careful with fire. The grass can be dry, and once ignited, it could burn for several kilometers.

The numerous huts on these mountains keep the human impact confined to small spots. These volcanoes are able to withstand a much greater human impact because of these shelters. Instead of 100 different permanent camping scars, there are only a few messy spots. Considering the number of climbers who visit these huts, it is surprising that there isn't more litter. Most visitors seem cognizant of this problem, but there are a few "bad seeds." Please pack out your own litter and that of your predecessors.

Most of the streams above 4000 m (13,000') are reasonably pure and probably fit to drink. To ensure that they remain that way, bury human waste in a shallow hole at least 90 m (300') away from any water supply, hut, or other campsite. Don't wash dishes in any streams. Don't pollute the streams with soap, detergents, or other substances.

Don't deface trees, rocks, or other natural features. Leave plants, animal life, and archaeological sites for others to enjoy.

[Top left] *Approaching Glaciar de Jamapa, El Pico de Orizaba, in gloomy weather (Rich Weber photo).* [Below] *View of Popocatepetl from Ixta rest stop (R.J. Secor photo)*

Please, don't destroy the mountain huts. Shut doors and windows before leaving. Once someone left the door to a hut open, and the next morning there was a layer of ice on the floor; I had to put on crampons just to cook breakfast.

At the risk of offending dog lovers, I am asking them to leave their canines at home. Dogs do not enjoy the same status in Mexico as they do in the United States. Most Mexicans view them as pests, and they are treated as such. Mexicans can't understand why people from the United States feed dogs good food and let them drink *agua purificado*. If you love your dog, leave Fido at home.

GETTING OUT OF MEXICO CITY

Mexico City is one of the largest cities in the world. Aside from human population, the city has grown at the rate of 400 new cars *per day* since 1968. In the downtown area, the streets are like four-lane parking lots during most of the day and early evening hours. The names of streets seem to change with every block, and one-way streets seem to change direction with every other block. It may take 20 minutes to get through a major intersection. It has taken me six hours to drive from Veracruz to Mexico City, and another two hours to drive the 10 km (6.2 mi) from the outskirts of the city to my home in the city. It would appear that the hardest part of climbing the volcanoes is navigating through Mexico City.

Purchase a map of the city, and attempt to find a way out of the maze. This advice may seem simple, but many tourists neglect to arm themselves with this essential tool.

For points east of Mexico City (including Popocatepetl, Iztaccihuatl, Orizaba, and Malinche) get on the major toll road leading east: Highway 190-D. This highway begins near the Mexico City airport. From the airport terminal, drive to the Avenida Puerto Aereo ("Airport Avenue"), and turn left (south). If you turn right, you may end up on the Circuito Interior, an urban freeway. After a few blocks you will come to a major street, Calzada I. Zaragoza (Ejercitio de Oriente) or Highway 190-D. Turn left (east), and you are headed toward the volcanoes. If you miss this street and head too far south, you will pass the Ciudad Deportiva, a huge gymnasium used during the 1968 Olympics.

If your destination is Nevado de Toluca or Nevado de Colima near Guadalajara, take Highway 15 west. From downtown Mexico City, take the Paseo de la Reforma west. After passing through Chapultepec Park, you will pass a monument commemorating the nationalization of the oil companies, which occurred in 1938. Shortly after this, you will drive through the Las Lomas area of the city, with such street names as "Chimborazo," "Aconcagua," "Sierra Negra," "Torrecillas," "Cotopaxi," "Monte Blanco," "Alpes," and "Himalaya." Stay on the Reforma until it becomes the Carreterra a Toluca.

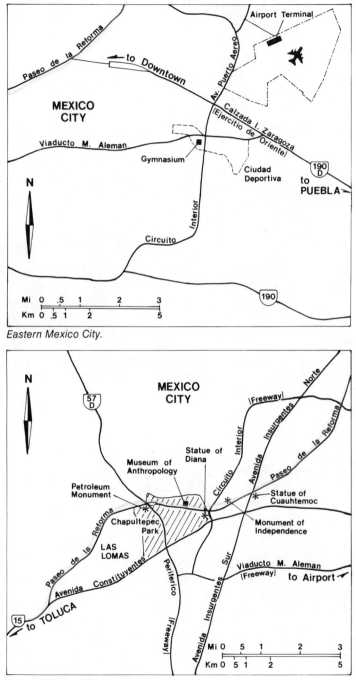

Eastern Mexico City.

Western Mexico City

Popocatepetl from Amecameca (Ray Smutek photo)

CHAPTER THREE

POPOCATEPETL AND IZTACCIHUATL

Most foreign climbers visit these two volcanoes first, and the Popo-Ixta National Park is a popular destination for families on day outings from the capital. The mountains are about 80 km (50 mi) from Mexico City, and it is not unusual for local *alpinistas* to climb either mountain in a day outing from the capital.

From Mexico City take Highway 190-D, headed southeast toward Puebla. At the first toll station, pull over to the far right-hand booth; there is a sign over it reading "Cuautla" (a nearby town). Pay the toll and then drive parallel to the highway for several kilometers. Leave the road at Highway

115-South. After passing through Chalco, Cedral, and San Rafael, you'll reach Amecameca.

Bottled water can be purchased in Amecameca. Market day is Sunday, and some climbing equipment may be for sale. From the plaza, a taxi service will take you to the lodge at Tlamacas for an impressive fee; and with a bit of bargaining, it may even take you to some of the other roadheads. You can purchase food and water and other last minute items in Amecameca before driving to Tlamacas.

If driving from Acapulco, Taxco, or Cuernavaca, it is much easier to drive directly to Amecameca, rather than driving through Mexico City. Take Highway 115-D, which leaves Highway 95-D approximately 20 km (12.4 mi) north of Cuernavaca. This toll road ends in a junction with Highway 115, south of Amecameca. This is a pleasant drive through the mountains.

From Amecameca, drive south on Highway 115. After 1 km (.6 mile), there is an intersection with signs pointing the way to Popo-Ixta National Park. Turn left and drive the 24 km (14.9 mi) of curving road to Paso de Cortés at 3650 m (12,000′). This is the low point between Popo and Ixta. Cortés first crossed this pass, and from here he saw the city of Tenochtitlán. A monument commemorates this event.

It is possible to reach the Paso de Cortés directly from Puebla. A dirt

road leads to the pass from Cholula, a town west of Puebla. The road is in fairly good condition and offers a direct route to Puebla for those wishing to visit El Pico de Orizaba after Ixta and Popo.

From Paso de Cortés, a dirt road leads north to the La Joya roadhead for Ixta. If bound for Popocatepetl, follow the paved road that leads south from the pass. There is a camping area about 2 km (1.2 mi) up the road from the pass, but there are no facilities except for a few fireplaces; water and toilets are absent.

Another kilometer (.6 mi) up the road at Tlamacas (3950 m; 12,950'), there are two lodges. The newer one is the magnificent Vincente Guerrero Lodge, completed in late 1978. I believe that "magnificent" is a just word, for the closest thing I have seen that would resemble it in the United States would be the Timberline Lodge on Mount Hood. Beds with blankets and sheets are available, along with flush toilets and hot showers for a nominal fee; the rate is extremely low by U.S. standards. There is a cafeteria on the premises, as well as a bar and two lounges with fireplaces. The staff of the lodge will watch your gear for you while you are away climbing. Adjacent to the lodge is a building that houses the Socorro Alpino de México. They usually are in attendance over the weekends, and it would be prudent to register your climb with them. Tap water in the lodge is reported to be safe to drink, but should be purified anyway.

Most foreigners use the Vincente Guerrero Lodge, and most Mexicans use the old lodge north of the newer building. A bunk costs very little, but toilet facilities and good water are absent. Crampons and ice axes can be rented here.

Don't leave any valuables overnight in an automobile, even a locked one, left in the lodges' parking lot. This includes items locked in the trunk. Either have a non-climber guard equipment while the rest of the party is away, or carry it inside the lodge and have the staff watch it. Never leave anything unattended inside the lodge.

In addition to climbing the volcanoes, there are numerous hikes in the vicinity. Day hikers can take the trail leading to Las Cruces, or the more ambitious can hike to the Queretano hut on the Ventorrillo route on Popocatepetl. The area surrounding Ixta provides many pleasant excursions. From La Joya there are two trails leading across the west side of the mountain; one leads to the Chalchoapan hut, which lies directly beneath "the neck" of Ixta. There are several trails leading to Amecameca from the meadows on the western slope of the mountain. Check the map before embarking on a hike, since many canyons have cliffs that are not always visible from above. Since it is easier to hike downhill than uphill, most hikers will want to start the hike from La Joya and finish at Amecameca. Most Mexicans do not like backpacking, as practiced in the States; when it comes to mountains, they are interested only in visiting the summits.

[Top right] *Vincente Guerrero Lodge, Tlamacas, with Popo in background*
[Below] *Interior of lodge (Ray Smutek photos)*

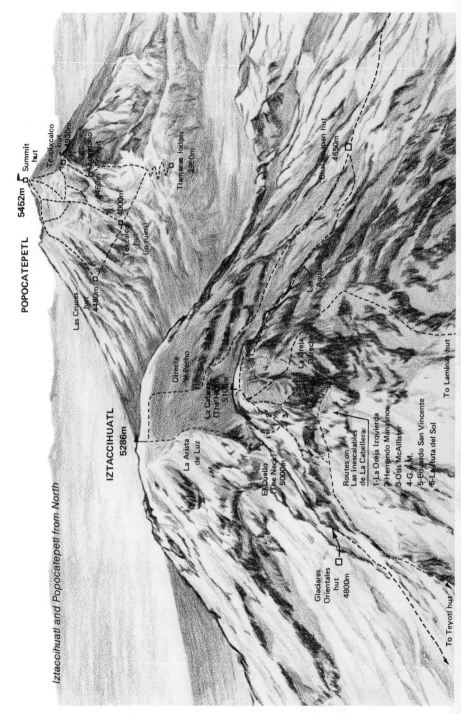

[Above] Popo from Iztaccihuatl. The Iglú hut can be seen to the far right and "the feet" to the left. (R.J. Secor photo)

Iztaccihuatl and Popocatepetl from North

POPOCATEPETL 5452m

Summit hut

Tlalmacas lodges 3950m

Tlamacas hut 4600m

Tropixcalco hut 4930m

Teopixcalco hut (in ruins)

4000m

Las Cruces hut 4480m

Chalchoapan hut 4650m

IZTACCIHUATL 5286m

Directa al Pecho

La Cabeza (The Head) 5100m

La Oreja Directa

Las Aguja

La Arista de Luz

El Cuello (The Neck) 5000m

Routes on Las Inescalables de La Cabellera:
1- La Oreja Izquierda
2- Hernando Manzanos
3- Otis McAllister
4- G.A.M.
5- Eduardo San Vincente
6- La Ruta del Sol

Glaciares Orientales hut 4800m

To Lamiñas hut

To Teyotl hut

[Above] *Popocatepetl from above Tlamacas*
[Right] *Las Cruces hut, Popo, with Ixta in background (Rich Weber photos)*

CLIMBING ROUTES ON POPOCATEPETL

Las Cruces ("The Crosses"). This is the most popular route on the mountain, having been climbed by persons wearing *huaraches* and by burros (the latter's footwear has been left unrecorded). I once climbed the peak and was followed by a dog all the way to the summit. On the other hand, once I saw a climber who thought it would be easier to descend the route by glissading. He lost control and slid quite a distance before the scree at the base of the peak stopped him. Snow conditions can vary between powder snow and glare ice. White-outs and cloud caps are common; so Popo demands respect, even in the best of conditions.

From Tlamacas, follow a well-defined trail that leads east along the base of the volcano. This trail could be called a "road," and it is easy to follow before sunrise. The trail ends at the Las Cruces hut (4480 m; 14,698′), approximately 500 m (1640′) above and 3 km (1.9 mi) from Tlamacas. This hike takes about two hours. Some parties spend the night at the Las Cruces hut in order to shorten the next day's ascent. But in recent years the hut has been in disrepair, and many day hikers visit the hut; so this has become a less favorable tactic.

From Las Cruces, the directions to the summit are simple: climb straight

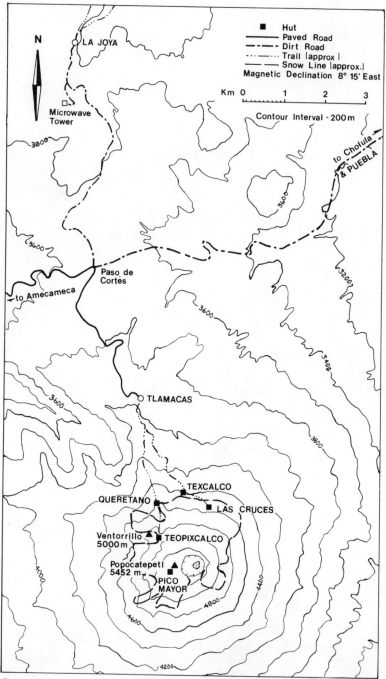

Popocatepetl

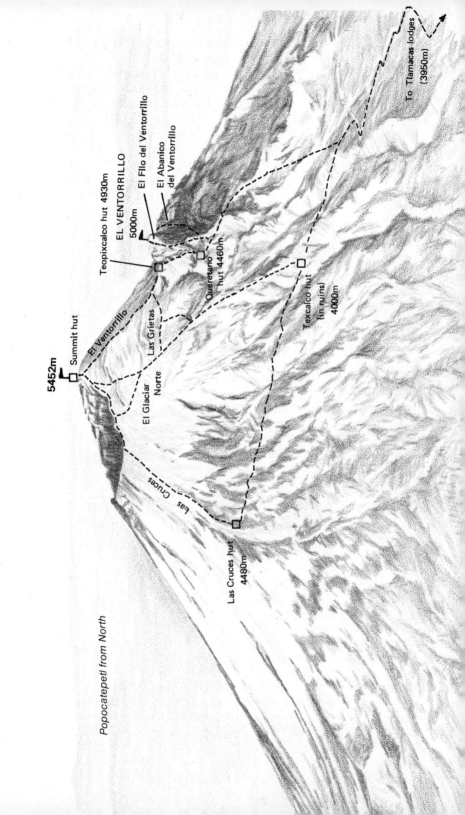

Popocatepetl from North

5452m
Summit hut

El Ventorrillo

El Glaciar Norte

Las Grietas

Las Cruces

Teopixcalco hut 4930m

EL VENTORRILLO
5000m

El Filo del Ventorrillo

El Abanico
del Ventorrillo

Queretano hut 4460m

Texcalco hut
(in ruins)
4000m

Las Cruces hut
4480m

To Tlamacas lodges
(3950m)

up the 30° slopes until the crater rim is reached. One usually has to negotiate a band of scree above the hut until axes and crampons become useful. Upon arrival at the crater rim, turn right, and after 45 minutes or so, the shelter that marks the Pico Mayor ("true summit") comes into view. The ascent should take from five to eight hours from Tlamacas.

The central attraction of Popocatepetl's summit is the crater. The crater rim is elliptical, with the long axis measuring 870 m (2850') and the short axis measuring 620 m (2035'); the circumference is 2300 m (7546'). The high point is on the west side of the crater, and from here the crater measures 480 m (1575') deep. The walls of the crater are nearly vertical, and there are several small volcanic cones and a small lake on the crater floor. Several fumaroles dot the floor, wall, and rim of the crater; and often their fumes make an extended stay on the summit uncomfortable. In 1921, a small spatter cone formed on the floor of the crater; this was the last significant volcanic activity. At one time there was a sulfur mining operation in the crater, with the miners climbing the peak daily, and then being lowered from the rim by means of a capstan. However, a tragic accident brought this operation to a quick end.

El Glaciar Norte ("The North Glacier"). On the north side of Popo a large group of crevasses can be seen. This route follows the snow and ice slope to the left of these crevasses. About 2.5 km (1.6 mi) from Tlamacas along the trail leading to Las Cruces lie the ruins of the Texcalco hut. From the hut, hike to the terminus of the glacier, a narrow tongue of ice to the right of a broad curving rock band. Above the snout, the slope averages 40°. Once above the level of the crevasses, the crater rim can be reached by any number of routes. Ropes and prusik slings are recommended due to the possibility of hidden crevasses.

Las Grietas ("The Crevasses"). This illogical route leads directly to the crevasses mentioned under the North Glacier route. However, it apparently contains the steepest ice climbing on the mountain. Follow the Glaciar Norte route to the vicinity of the snout of the glacier. Traverse right, around a curved ridge to the next glacier to the west. (Some may be tempted to approach this glacier directly from the canyon beneath it; this approach is not recommended.) Surmount the snout of the glacier; the easiest route depends on the snow and ice conditions. Above the snout, climb straight up to the huge crevasses. From here, either traverse left (east) to the Las Cruces or Glaciar Norte routes, or traverse right (west) to the Ventorrillo route. If conditions allow it, zigzag through the crevasses and climb directly to the crater rim. Crevasse rescue equipment should be carried.

El Ventorrillo. This is the preferred route for climbers of intermediate experience. It is the most direct route from Tlamacas and is located in a spectacu-

[Top right] *The summit of Popo from the top of the Las Cruces route (Rich Weber photo).* [Below] *El Glaciar Norte, Popo (Ray Smutek photo)*

[Above] *Popocatepetl from Paso de Cortés (Rich Weber photo)*

El Ventorrillo from North

5000m

El Filo
del Ventorrillo

El Abanico
del Ventorrillo

Queretano
hut

4460m

To Tlamacas

lar and exhilarating setting. There are two huts on the route, and even though they are not really needed due to the proximity of the roadhead, they offer the opportunity to sleep high on the mountain with tremendous views from their balconies. For those who are more than "peak baggers," this is the way to go. (It would appear that this is the route that the conquistadors followed.)

From Tlamacas, take the Las Cruces trail until a smaller trail forks off to the right at approximately 4100 m (13,450'). This trail leads to the northeast ridge of the Ventorrillo. From the ridge, the trail leads to the Queretano hut at 4460 m (14,632'). This hut is located on a spectacular, overhanging cliff overlooking the canyon that separates the Ventorrillo from the glaciers of Popocatepetl; it would be an interesting and comfortable place to spend the night. Above the "cliff hut" the route remains on the canyon side of the northeast ridge of the Ventorrillo. Avoid dropping into the canyon; it is much better to stay high on the shelf between the cliffs of the Ventorrillo and the cliffs of the canyon. The Teopixcalco hut is located at the saddle at 4930 m (16,175'). Those wishing to climb the Ventorrillo will find it a short scramble from the saddle. Rope up at the saddle, and climb directly to the main peak. The slope averages 35°, with occasional stretches at 45°. The angle lessens to the left, but more crevasses are encountered. Farther to the right there are fewer crevasses, but the angle steepens considerably. (The west face of the mountain is an impressive 45° slope, which always seems to be glare ice. There have been several ascents of the west face; the principal difficulty is the approach. It may be best to traverse from the Teopixcalco hut.) Between five and seven hours after leaving Tlamacas, the smell of sulfur will become apparent, and the summit should be nearby.

El Filo del Ventorrillo ("The Ridge of the Ventorrillo"). The northeast ridge of the Ventorrillo is marked by a deep gap. Take the trail that leads to the Ventorrillo route and continue up the ridge leading to the summit of the Ventorrillo. The gap is negotiated by means of interesting downclimbing and rappels. Regain the ridge on the other side of the gap and follow it to the summit. Hard hats, ropes, and hardware should be taken on this class 4-5 climb.

El Abanico del Ventorrillo ("The Palisade of the Ventorrillo"). There are several class 5 rock climbing routes on the northwest face. Approach the base of this face by means of the trail for the Ventorrillo route. Before reaching the northeast ridge, several rock outcroppings can be seen on the ridge leading north. Hike up to the top of these rocks and traverse right, atop the higher of the two prominent rock bands leading across the base of the cliff. From here, at least four routes have been done. All of the routes avoid the summit headwall by traversing around to the west or south sides of the summit. Full rock climbing impedimenta are necessary, perhaps crampons and ice axes too.

[Top right] *Approaching the Queretano hut on the Ventorrillo route, Popo*
[Below] *The Teopixcalco hut, Popocatepetl, with Ixta in background*
(R.J. Secor photos)

[Left] *The Queretano hut, Popo.* [Top] *Las Grietas, Popocatepetl*
[Below] *The summit of Popo from the Teopixcalco hut (Ray Smutek photos)*

[Left] *Traversing the crater rim of Popo, Las Cruces route (Rich Weber photo)* [Top] *The summit of Popocatepetl (R.J. Secor photo).* [Below] *The summit hut of Popocatepetl (R.J. Secor photo)*

[Above] On the summit of Popo, with Ixta in background (Rich Weber photo)
[Below] The crater of Popocatepetl (Rich Weber photo)

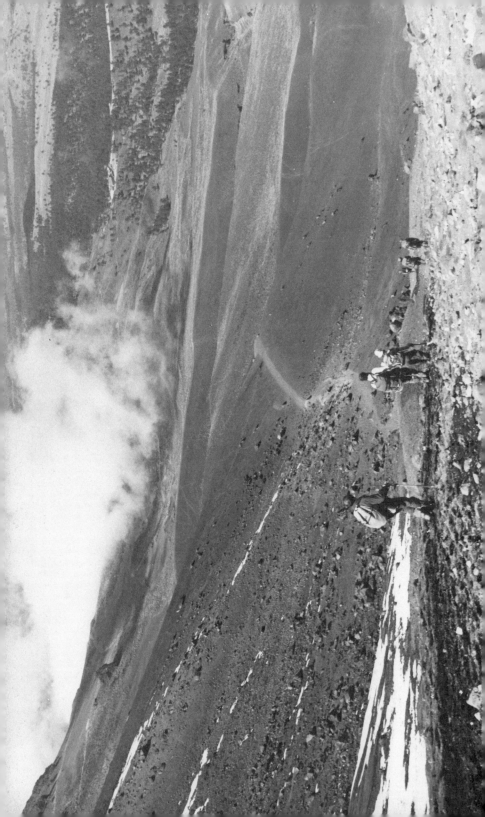

[Above] Descending Las Cruces route, Tlamacas in right background (Rich Weber photo). [Below] Popocatepetl from Paso de Cortes (Ray Smutek photo)

CLIMBING ROUTES ON IZTACCIHUATL

Ixta is my favorite of the three volcanoes. Although the standard route is long, it offers some route-finding difficulties and much more interest than the normal routes on Popo or Orizaba. Since the standard route is a traverse along many false summits and broad snowfields, as opposed to climbing straight up a volcanic cone, it is easy to get disoriented in a white-out. Prudent climbers will take bearings and mark the route with wands to ensure a certain and safe return.

According to Aztec mythology, Iztaccihuatl is known as the "sleeping lady," as can readily be seen when viewing the mountain from the west. The following terms for the parts of the mountain are in common use:

La Cabellera: the hair
La Cabeza: the head
La Oreja: the ear
El Cuello: the neck
El Pecho: the breast
La Barriga: the belly
Las Rodillas: the knees
Los Pies: the feet

Ixta is climbed from two major roadheads: La Joya (4000 m; 13,124') from Paso de Cortés, and Nexcoalanco (3600 m; 11,811') from the town of San Rafael, north of Amecameca.

La Joya is reached easily by means of a dirt road from Paso de Cortés. Many assume that the road ends at the microwave station, but it continues northward another 1.5 km (.9 mi) to the parking area. This is the roadhead leading to the three huts below "the knees," and the huts on the western side of the mountain, the Ayoloco and Chalchoapan huts. La Joya has a bad reputation among climbers when the conversation turns to thieves.

Nexcoalanco is harder to reach, but it offers the quickest means to approach the routes on "the head." Highway 115 goes through Tlalmanalco before arriving at Amecameca. From the center of Tlalmanalco, drive approximately 6 km (3.7 mi) east to the village of San Rafael. From here a steep, rough road climbs uphill to Nexcoalanco, where a climber's hut is located. Many climbers hire transportation in San Rafael or Amecameca to take them to Nexcoalanco. Others leave their vehicles in San Rafael and hike the 6 km (3.7 mi) to the hut.

Another approach to the northern side of Ixta utilizes a road that begins at Pueblo Nuevo, a village halfway between Tlalmanalco and San Rafael. The road climbs north from Pueblo Nuevo, and passes above San Rafael. After passing through a forest with many switchbacks, the road ends with a "T" intersection (8.7 km; 5.4 mi from Pueblo Nuevo). Turn right, go through some more switchbacks, and 3.5 km (2.2 mi) after the intersection, a trail leaves the road to the right; 2 km (1.2 mi) farther lies Nexcoalanco. Another

At the Portillo, Iztaccihuatl (R.J. Secor photo)

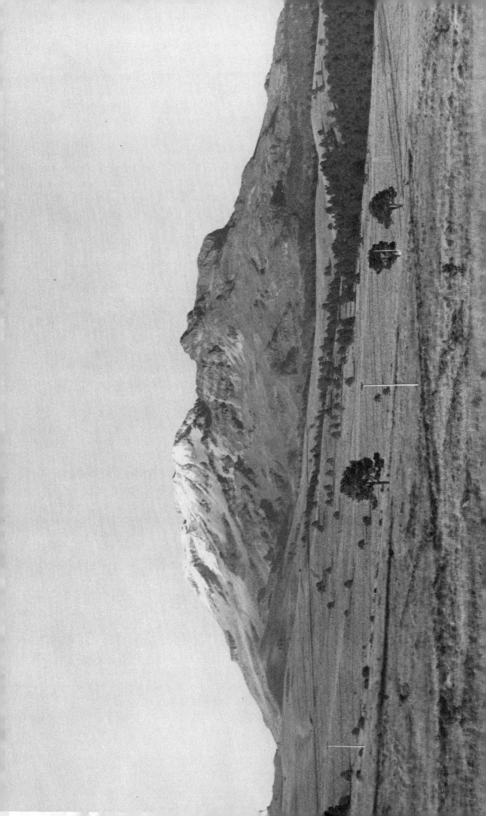

[Above] Iztaccihuatl from Paso de Cortés (Rich Weber photo)

Iztaccihuatl from West

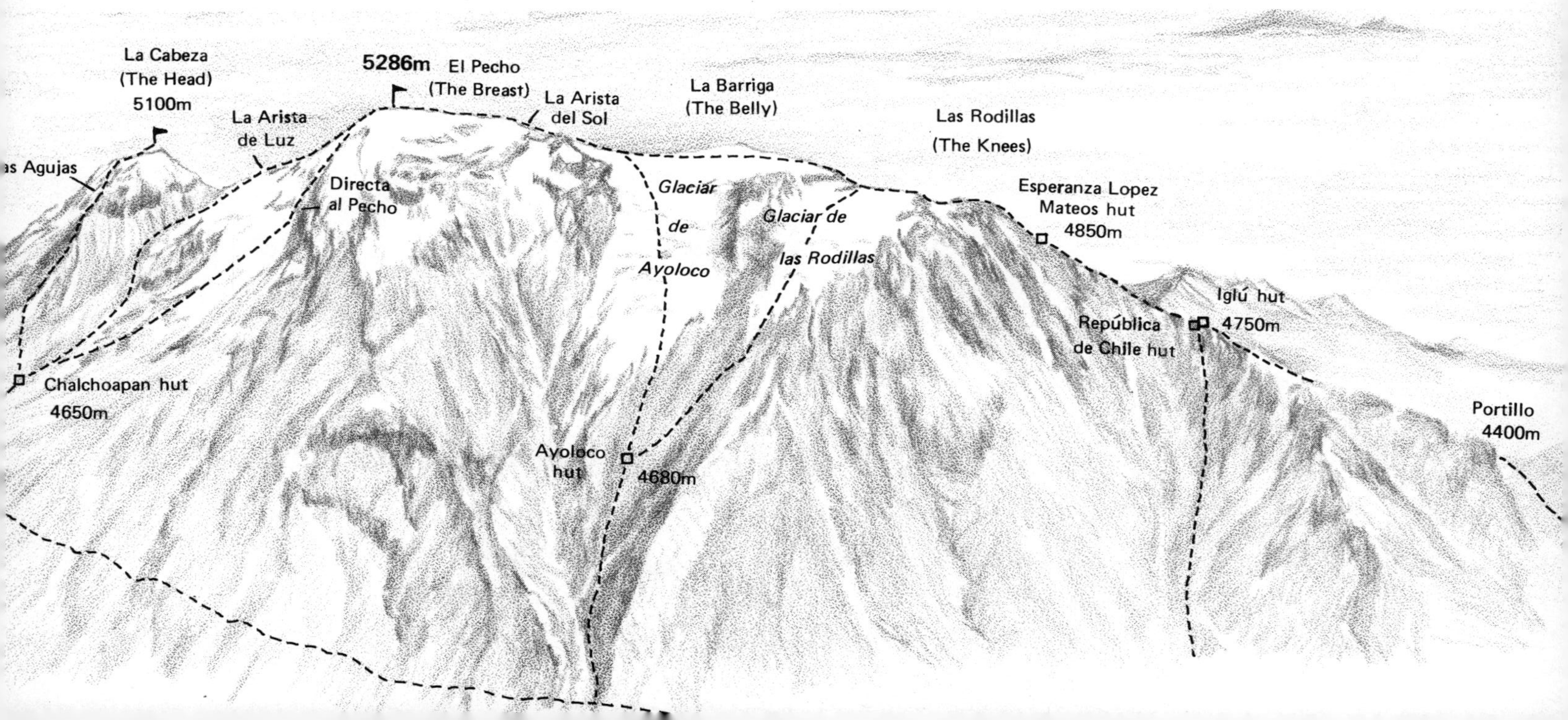

La Cabeza
(The Head)
5100m

Las Agujas

La Arista
de Luz

5286m El Pecho
(The Breast)

La Arista
del Sol

Directa
al Pecho

Chalchoapan hut
4650m

La Barriga
(The Belly)

Glaciar
de
Ayoloco

Glaciar de
Glaciar de
las Rodillas

Las Rodillas
(The Knees)

Esperanza Lopez
Mateos hut
4850m

Ayoloco
hut

4680m

República
de Chile hut

Iglú hut
4750m

Portillo
4400m

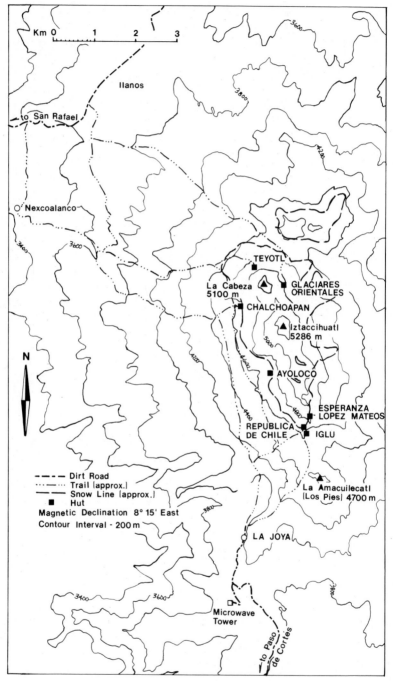

Km 0   1   2   3

llanos

to San Rafael

Nexcoalanco

N

TEYOTL

La Cabeza
5100 m

GLACIARES
ORIENTALES

CHALCHOAPAN

Iztaccihuatl
5286 m

AYOLOCO

ESPERANZA
LOPEZ MATEOS

REPUBLICA
DE CHILE

IGLU

- - - Dirt Road
· · · Trail (approx.)
— Snow Line (approx.)
■ Hut
Magnetic Declination 8° 15' East
Contour Interval - 200 m

La Amacuilecatl
(Los Pies) 4700 m

LA JOYA

Microwave
Tower

to Paso
de Cortes

Iztaccihuatl

The Head and Breast of Iztaccihuatl from West

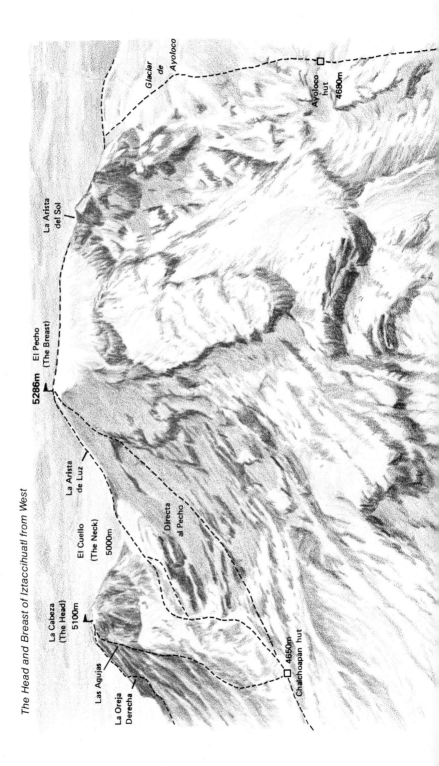

La Cabeza
(The Head)
5100m

La Oreja
Derecha

Las Agujas

El Cuello
(The Neck)
5000m

La Arista
de Luz

Directa
al Pecho

4650m
Chalchoapan hut

5286m El Pecho
(The Breast)

La Arista
del Sol

Glaciar
de
Ayoloco

Ayoloco
hut
4680m

kilometer farther on the main road, a large, flat *llano* ("plain") is reached and a trail leads toward the northern side of "the head" of Ixta.

Of the two roadheads, Nexcoalanco and La Joya, I prefer La Joya due to its simple approach and higher elevation. Most of the routes can be approached from this roadhead quite easily. Many years ago there was a small hut located here, but it has long since disappeared.

Rising above La Joya is a subsidiary peak of Iztaccihuatl, La Amacuilecatl (also known as Los Pies or "the feet"). From the cars, a trail leads straight uphill toward a cliff. After a short distance it angles left, gradually gaining elevation until the saddle between "the knees" and "the feet," the Portillo ("pass"), is reached. Before arriving at the Portillo, the trail crosses a saddle at approximately 4400 m (14,436'); a landmark for this saddle is a castle-like rock formation just to the left when facing toward the main summit of Ixta. Many climbers bound for "the knees" huts have lost the trail and climbed over the top of this formation; minimum class 3. Climb the ridge that rises above this saddle to the summit. Another route on La Amacuilecatl starts at the Portillo, but soon leaves the ridge and traverses onto the northeast face. Both routes are class 3-4. In the vicinity of La Joya, there are several other cliffs and crags that have seen roped ascents. The rock is not especially bad, and it would be an interesting place to spend a free afternoon.

La Arista del Sol ("The Ridge of the Sun"). In the 1920s and 1930s a climber, Francisco Soto de Arroyo, pioneered some of the more difficult routes on the volcanoes, and gave unique names to the characteristics of their physical features. This name refers to the final ridge leading to the summit. (Nevertheless, most climbers refer to this route as "the knees" route.)

This is the standard route on the mountain, and since the nature of the climb is much different from climbs on the other volcanoes, this route is an enjoyable change. With Popo to one's back and El Pico de Orizaba to the east, the setting is exhilarating.

Between "the knees" and "the breast," four false summits are encountered. It is easy to get lost on these long flat snowfields; keep an eye on the clouds, take bearings, and mark your route of ascent. Another complication is the difficulty in retreating in the event of bad weather or altitude illness. It is tempting to make a quick descent to the west, but several cliffs and icefalls hamper the escape; this should be attempted only by those who are familiar with the mountain. It is best to descend Ixta via the route of ascent.

Most people take two days to climb Ixta, spending a night in one of the three huts below "the knees." However, the peak can be climbed quite easily in a day from La Joya, and this may be preferable if there is an absence of snow on the peak. There is no running water at the huts, and sometimes there is not enough snow to melt for water.

[Top right] *The Chalchoapan hut, Ixta. This hut is located below "the neck."*
[Below] *Early morning on La Arista del Sol, Iztaccihuatl. Esperanza Lopez Mateos hut in upper left-hand corner. (R.J. Secor photos)*

There are two approaches to the huts. One involves hiking the trail that leads to the Portillo from the parking area (see description for "the feet"). From the Portillo, the trail stays on the eastern slope of the ridge, gradually climbing back onto the ridge before the huts are reached. It is necessary to climb over a small peak, and then drop 35 m (120') to get to the two lower of the three huts, the Iglú and República de Chile (4750 m; 15,585'). The third hut is higher, located just below the prominent rock band of "the knees"; the Esperanza Lopez Mateos refuge is at 4850 m (15,912'). It takes from four to six hours to hike to these huts from La Joya.

The other approach to "the knees" huts involves hiking up the western slope below the huts. From La Joya, a trail leads north and slightly downhill across a wide, grassy valley. The trail then climbs to a small saddle. From the saddle, turn right and start climbing uphill, and by passing a prominent cliff to the right, the three huts can be reached. There are also several trails that traverse across the western slope of the mountain. The most prominent trail continues northward from the saddle north of La Joya, and leads to the Chalchoapan huts. Another trail traverses high on the western side of the mountain from "the knees" huts to the Ayoloco hut. This higher trail is rather faint, and most climbers will undoubtedly lose it.

Above the huts, it is necessary to negotiate the cliff that marks "the knees." The preferred way involves climbing the snow on the left side of the cliff, but often there is not enough snow to cover the scree adequately. Should this be the case, it is better to climb the class 2-3 rocks to the right. From the top of the Rodillas, climb over the several false summits to the anticlimactic snowdome that marks the apex of the seventh highest peak of North America. The ascent takes four to six hours from the huts. Ice axes and crampons should be carried, but may not be needed.

Glaciar de las Rodillas ("The Knees Glacier"). This route starts at the Ayoloco hut (4690 m; 15,387'), beneath the Ayoloco Glacier on the western side of the mountain. This hut can be reached either by traversing from "the knees" huts, or by climbing up from one of the trails that traverses on the west side of the mountain. Above the Ayoloco hut there are two glaciers, separated by a *rognon* (a large kidney-shaped rock). To the right of these rocks is the Glaciar de las Rodillas, and the route climbs directly up this glacier, zigzagging through crevasses. Near the top, traverse to the left toward the Pecho, where a long walk leads to the summit. The angle averages 45°; and axes, crampons, ropes and crevasse rescue equipment should be carried.

Glaciar de Ayoloco ("Ayoloco Glacier"). This is believed to be the route of the first ascent of Ixta, first climbed by James de Salis in 1889. From the Ayoloco hut, climb straight up the glacier. Crevasses and small ice-cliffs may bar the way, but can easily be passed. No false summits are encountered, and for climbers of moderate experience, this is a preferable route to "the knees" route.

Between Las Rodillas and La Barriga on Ixta (R.J. Secor photo)

Directa al Pecho ("Direct to the Breast"). This route climbs the northwest face of the main summit, "the breast." At first glance, it appears to be a straightforward, 700 m (2300′) 40° snow-and-ice climb, but several obstacles are not visible when viewing the face from the Chalchoapan huts. Several small ice cliffs bar the way low on the face, and the angle steepens appreciably 250 m (800′) below the summit. Here a rock band bars the way, and it is necessary to pass to the left. Many intimidated parties traverse to "The Ridge of Light" to finish the climb.

La Arista de Luz ("The Ridge of Light"). This route is also called El Cuello or "the neck" route, but Francisco Soto's imaginative name is used here.

From Nexcoalanco a trail leads around a ridge to Cañada Nahualac. The trail switchbacks at 3700 m (12,150′), but another trail continues up the canyon, crosses a ridge, and then continues uphill to the Chalchoapan huts, located at 4600 m (15,100′), on the moraine of the glacier leading to "the neck." Chalchoapan can also be reached from La Joya by means of the trail leading across the western slope of Ixta.

From Chalchoapan, hike across the moraine to the glacier, then climb to the saddle ("the neck") between "the head" and the main summit; the angle averages 30°. From "the neck," "the head" is a short distance away; a short class 3 section must be negotiated. The Arista de Luz leads to the main summit from "the neck" and offers little difficulty; but beware of crevasses, which cross this ridge.

Las Agujas ("The Needles"). Looking north from Chalchoapan, a ridge can be seen leading to "the head." On the lower portion of this ridge, there are several pinnacles, which are often climbed for their own sake. It is possible to bypass the needles completely and climb directly up the slopes leading to the summit of "the head."

La Oreja Derecha ("The Right Ear"). A more appropriate name for this route might be "The Right Temple and Forehead." This route climbs the northwest flank of "the head." For this and the following routes, the usual approach is from the *llanos* north of the mountain. It is possible to reach this side of the mountain from the Chalchoapan huts. A trail leads north from Chalchoapan across the lower ridge of Las Agujas and then drops 200 m (650′). There is a hut located in this area. Traverse across the lower slopes of "the head," then climb up the scree to the snow. A permanent snowfield descends from the summit between two bands of rock. Climb the snowfield, about 45°, then climb to the summit of "the head" by any number of routes.

Las Inescalables de La Cabellera ("The Unclimbable Routes of the Hair"). This does not refer to any specific route, but rather to the collection of routes on the northeastern side of "the head." A trail from the *llanos* north of Ixta leads to the saddle northeast of "the head." From the saddle, it is possible to reach the Glaciares Orientales hut. By continuing up the ridge from the saddle, the Teyotl hut is reached. The northeast ridge itself leads to the class 4-5 rock routes on "the head." The ridge is mostly scree and tedious hiking. Underneath the northeast face, the ridge ends in a rock buttress. Traverse across the right side of the buttress, and surmount it on its northern side. From here three routes present themselves. La Oreja Izquierda ("The Left Ear") traverses across the face to the left, and then climbs the east ridge of "the head." The Hernando Manzanos Route (named after one of the climbers who died shortly after making its first ascent) climbs the face immediately above the buttress; this is the first route climbed on the Caballera (done in the mid-1950s). The Otis McAllister Route climbs farther to the right of the Manzanos Route. There are three routes on the far right-hand face; instead of climbing the aforementioned buttress, it is better to traverse across the face to reach their bases. The G.A.M. Route is named after the Grupo Alta Montaña (the High Mountain Group) of CEMAC. Eduardo San Vincente participated in five foreign expeditions before meeting with tragedy on Mount Victoria in the Canadian Rockies in 1954, and a route is named after him. Another route is known as La Ruta del Sol ("The Route of the Sun").

"The neck" can easily be reached from the east.

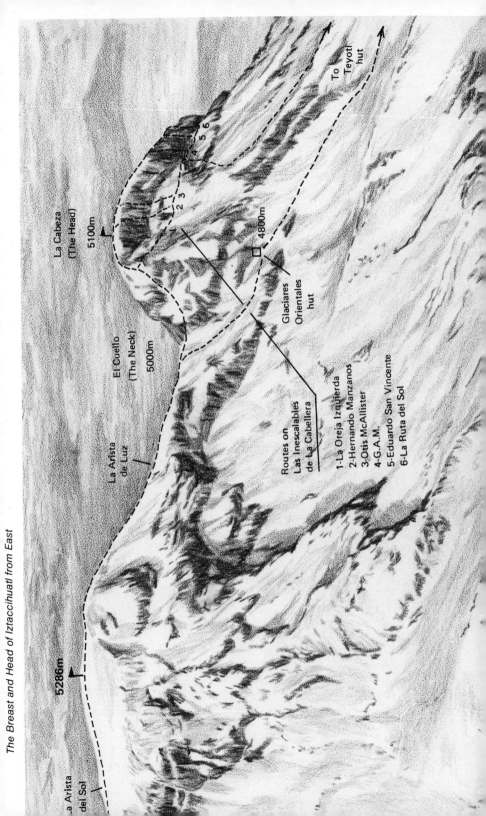

The Breast and Head of Iztaccihuatl from East

La Arista
del Sol

5286m

La Arista
de Luz

El Cuello
(The Neck)
5000m

La Cabeza
(The Head)
5100m

To
Teyotl
hut

Glaciares
Orientales hut

4800m

1
2
3

4
5
6

Routes on
Las Inescalables
de La Cabellera

1 – La Oreja Izquierda
2 – Hernando Manzanos
3 – Otis McAllister
4 – G.A.M.
5 – Eduardo San Vincente
6 – La Ruta del Sol

[Above] *La Arista del Sol, Ixta, above the Esperanza Lopez Mateos hut* (R.J. Secor photo)
[Below] *La Arista del Sol, Iztaccihuatl* (John Pollock photo)

[Above] Sunrise on Iztaccihuatl, Popocatepetl in background
[Below] La Arista del Sol, Iztaccihuatl (Herb Kincey photos)

El Pico de Orizaba from the north (R.J. Secor photo)

CHAPTER FOUR

EL PICO DE ORIZABA

Driving east on Highway 140 or 150-D from Puebla, one crosses the continental divide in the vicinity of Acatzingo. Those driving the toll highway from Puebla toward Veracruz (Highway 190-D) get off the highway approximately 40 km (24.9 mi) after Puebla. There is a sign here showing the turnoff to Highway 140, which leads to Jalapa. At the end of the off ramp, turn left, drive underneath the toll road, and after 2 km (1.2 mi), you'll arrive at the town of Acatzingo, where the market is held on Tuesdays. Highway 140 originates in Puebla and offers a scenic (and free) alternative to the toll road.

Another 27 km (16.8 mi) north on Highway 140 brings you to the town of El Seco. By turning right and traveling another 30 km (18.6 mi), Ciudad Serdan is reached. It was from here that most of the attempts on Orizaba

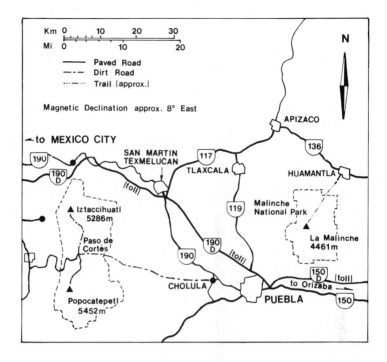

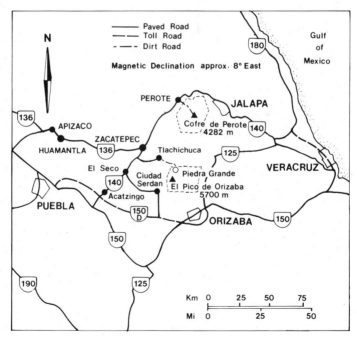

83

were made prior to the building of the road on the north side of the mountain. Market day is held on Sundays and Mondays, and food and lodging are available. One establishment, the Hotel Fausto, has been serving mountaineers for almost a hundred years.

Returning to El Seco and Highway 140, continue northward on the highway another 7 km (4.3 mi) to an intersection marked by a large, white P.R.I. sign, pointing the way to Tlachichuca. (The Partido Revolucionario Institucional is Mexico's largest political party.) Turn right, Tlachichuca is another 22 km (13.7 mi).

Rigo Thurmer described Tlachichuca as, "...the home of Señor Reyes' mountain empire." He continues:

> This enterprising gentleman has the climbing racket firmly sewed up. He owns the only gas station in town, as well as the only grocery store and the only telephone. He also owns the only two vehicles that can make it up to the Piedra Grande hut at 13,996' on Orizaba. We signed in at the unofficial climbing register at the grocery store. From some of the comments in the book we gathered that climbing Orizaba was not exactly a walk in the Black Forest. An ancient Dodge Power Wagon, which I thought was junked, turned out to be our vehicle. At 350 Pesos a head, it seemed to be rather spartan transportation. I had ample opportunity to change my mind later on—the truck had no muffler, manifold, fuel pump, hood, lights, windows, and no handbrakes.[1]

Mr. Thurmer's observations are not totally accurate, but they provide an adequate description of Tlachichuca.

Señor Reyes' store, La Antigua Flor, is across the street from the PEMEX station. Contact him for a place to spend the night in town, taxi service to the Piedra Grande ("Big Rock") huts, and a safe place to park your car while away hiking and climbing. Taxi rates vary with the amount of people and baggage transported, size of the vehicle used, and one's ability at bargaining. The road to Piedra Grande is a rough one, and it is not uncommon to get out and push the "taxi" over an occasional difficult section.

Some people have used their own, or rented, a two-wheel-drive vehicle to get to the roadhead. I have tried this myself and was successful, albeit with slight damage to my car. The road is extremely rough and bumpy. When it is dry, it is so dusty that it is difficult to see past the windshield, and when it is wet, the volcanic soil is very slick, and it is difficult to get traction. One party did it with a mini bus and sedan, and reported no trouble. Another chap did it with a small sedan and said that he wouldn't do it again. I would not advise driving a two-wheel drive vehicle to Piedra Grande, but a few people do it. If you get stuck, there is no auto club to free you. Good luck.

Others have elected to ignore the motor vehicle completely and have hiked the 21 km (13 mi) to the Piedra Grande huts. This appears to be a

---

[1]Rigo Thurmer, "Popo, Ixta and Orizaba," *Mountain Gazette*, No. 63 (Nov. 1977), p. 29.

pleasant hike, taking you through two villages and fields of corn and potatoes. The elevation gain from Tlachichuca to Piedra Grande is 1500 m (5000′).

For those driving to Piedra Grande, the following mileage log may be of use. It begins at the plaza at Tlachichuca.

TLACHICHUCA

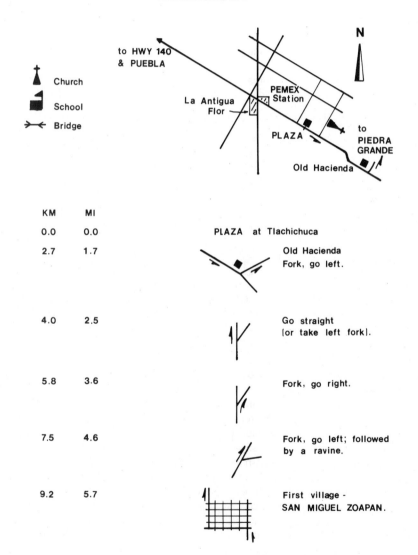

KM	MI	
0.0	0.0	PLAZA at Tlachichuca
2.7	1.7	Old Hacienda Fork, go left.
4.0	2.5	Go straight (or take left fork).
5.8	3.6	Fork, go right.
7.5	4.6	Fork, go left; followed by a ravine.
9.2	5.7	First village - SAN MIGUEL ZOAPAN.

KM	MI		
11.8	7.3		Fork, go right.
12.7	7.9		Road follows a prominent ravine.
14.1	8.7		Second village - MIGUEL HILDAGO Y COSTILLA. Turn left after bridge.
16.3	10.1		2 Forks; turn right twice. You are now on top of the ridge.
17.6	10.9		Fork, go right.
18.6	11.5		Very steep, may stop two – wheel drive vehicles. Can be done class 1 or class 6, depending on road condition and recent weather. Fortunately, there are 3 or 4 choices to follow. Stop, get out and look around. The best route may not be apparent at first. Keep trying; you'll make it.
21.0	13.0		PIEDRA GRANDE; elevation 4260 m (14,000 ft.)

Park your car *uphill* from the large stone shelter if possible. Some climbers have parked their cars facing downhill and have returned from their climb to find that someone had ripped off their cars by using the old push-start technique. For that matter, it is not recommended that gear be left unattended at Piedra Grande; numerous thefts have been reported.

There are two huts at Piedra Grande. The older structure, the Augusto Pellet hut, is made out of corrugated metal, and as many as 12 have fit into the various sleeping shelves. The newer hut, Octavio Alvarez, is a large stone structure with room for over 60 people. Before it was built in 1972, Piedra Grande was a "tent-city" at Christmas and over busy weekends. Many of the windows are broken, thus providing a convenient place to get rid of garbage; rubbish abounds beneath the windows. Considerate climbers will refrain from such practices and police the area around the hut. Señor Reyes will be happy to take any garbage off your hands. Those who patch

El Pico de Orizaba

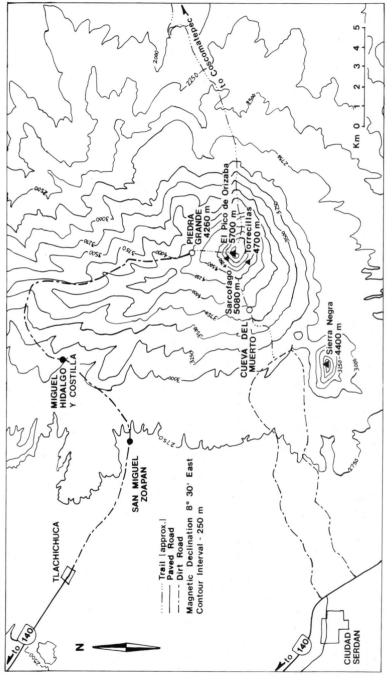

the windows with plastic or cardboard will be doing those who follow a real service.

There is no running water in the immediate vicinity of Piedra Grande. The closest water is uphill in a gully; depending on the season, the spring may or may not be running. The water from the spring can be used without purification.

There are numerous crosses and memorials surrounding the huts at Piedra Grande, commemorating those who have died on the slopes above.

CLIMBING ROUTES

Glaciar de Jamapa ("Jamapa Glacier"). This is now the standard route on the mountain; another name often used is *Ruta Norte*, or "Northern Route." From Piedra Grande, a well-worn trail leads to the right of a prominent gully. Pass a series of dark cliffs to the right, and once above these, hike up a bare, rocky valley to a flat area at approximately 4900 m (16,000'); some parties camp here to shorten the ascent. The glacier starts here, and it would be best to rope up, since many climbers have found several hidden crevasses. Continue climbing up the glacier, which at times is steep, to the rocks that mark the crater rim. Traverse underneath the rocks to the right for approximately 200 m (656'), then climb upward to the crater rim. Hike around the rim to the high point, marked by a cross. From high on the mountain, one can see the Gulf of Mexico to the east and easily sight Popo and Ixta to the west. The ascent should take six to nine hours from Piedra Grande.

Glaciar Oriental ("Eastern Glacier"). This route was made famous recently by an article that appeared in *Summit* magazine, a U.S. publication.[2] The eastern side of the mountain is characterized as having two couloirs. The southern, or left-hand couloir, has been described as having an angle of 70°, with the right-hand couloir being at 60°, but I am very skeptical about these reported slopes. The easiest approach is from Piedra Grande, by climbing the Jamapa Glacier route to approximately 5000 m (16,400'), and then traversing to the left (south) over a ridge to the basins beneath the two couloirs. It is also possible to traverse at a lower level directly from Piedra Grande, but the loose volcanic rocks and soil make the higher traverse over snow much more inviting. An alternative to the Piedra Grande approach involves hiking in from the town of Coscomatepec, 25 km (15.5 mi) to the east. With the use of burros, this seems to be an attractive alternative to the ruts, bumps, and washboards leading to the Piedra Grande huts.

From the top of the couloirs, traverse to the right or the northern half of the crater rim. There may be little or no snow on the southern half, making for

[2]Dan McCool, "Orizaba—The Other Side of the Mountain," *Summit*, Vol. 25, No. 3 (June-July 1979), pp. 9-11.

[Top right] *El Pico de Orizaba from Piedra Grande. Summit is in upper left-hand corner, Augusto Pellet hut in foreground (R.J. Secor photo).* [Below] *Octavio Alvarez hut, Piedra Grande, El Pico de Orizaba (R.J. Secor photo)*

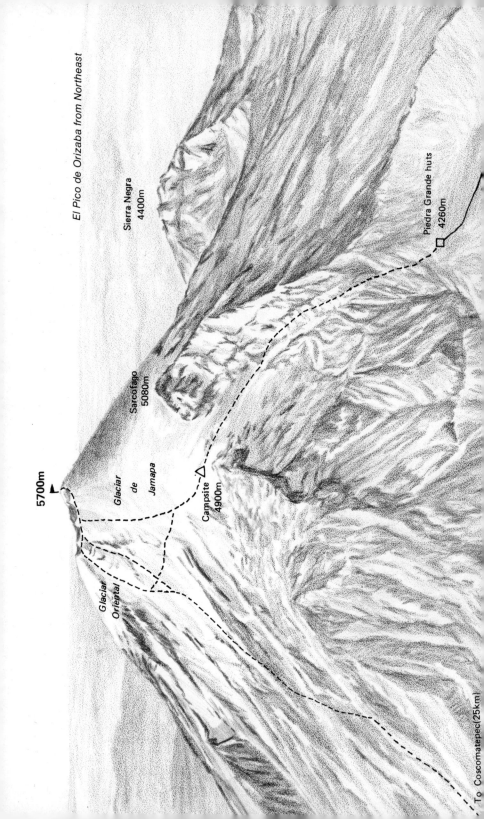

El Pico de Orizaba from Northeast

Sierra Negra
4400m

Piedra Grande huts
4260m

Sarcófago
5080m

5700m

Glaciar de Jamapa

Campsite
4900m

Glaciar Oriental

To Coscomatepec (25km)

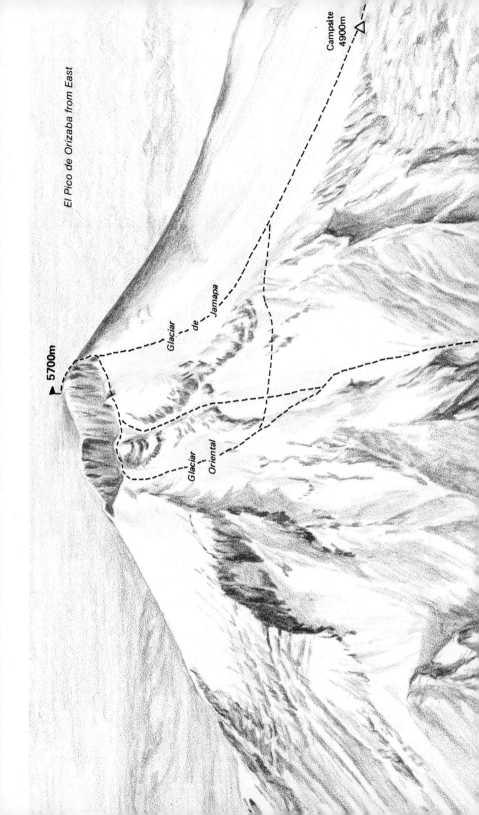

El Pico de Orizaba from East

5700m

Glaciar de Jamapa

Glaciar Oriental

Campsite 4900m

uncomfortable walking. From the summit, descend the Jamapa Glacier to 5200 m (17,000′) and traverse across the ridge leading to the basin beneath the two couloirs.

Climbers have also ascended on the southeast and the south sides, approaching the mountain from the city of Orizaba. But there is no permanent snow on this side of the mountain, and ascents from this side are not as attractive.

La Pared Norte ("The North Wall"). This route actually climbs the northwest face of the Sarcofago, a rocky, volcanic peak just north of the true summit of Orizaba. It was first climbed in September 1948 by a six-man party in marginal weather conditions. After approaching the base of the climb from the village of San Miguel Zoapan, they camped at approximately 4500 m (14,760′). The next morning they started the climb; and before long their clothes, ice axes, and ropes were covered with a thin layer of ice. Often, clouds, fog, and blowing snow obscured visibility, and their progress was slow. They reached the summit of Orizaba at nine o'clock that night, and at 1:30 the next morning arrived at the Cueva del Muerto, where they met their support party.

This side of Orizaba can be approached by taking any of the roads that leave the Piedra Grande road below the village of San Miguel Zoapan. It is probably easier to traverse to the base of the climb directly from Piedra Grande; this way it is easier to return to a base camp if making an alpine style climb. It is necessary to double back northward on this traverse to avoid the cliffs that mark the northwest side of the north ridge of the Sarcofago. One should allow a full day for this traverse. The principal obstacle on the face itself is a vertical rock band. This can be by-passed on the right, either by climbing the ramp that ascends to the left above the cliffs, or by climbing directly up the snow and ice couloirs to the right of the cliff. Above the face, climb up the glacier on the upper northwest side of the mountain; some may wish to traverse over to the Jamapa Glacier. Allow 9 to 12 hours for this climb from its base.

Ruta Sur Occidental ("Southwestern Route"). This was formerly the standard route on Orizaba, before the construction of the road to Piedra Grande in the early 1960s. There are two approaches that have been used. One involves hiking directly from Ciudad Serdan to Cueva del Muerto, the campsite, by means of pack trails; this is a pleasant 20-km (12.4-mi) hike, with 1800 m (5900′) of gain. The other approach offers less hiking and is thus preferable for those backpacking, instead of using pack animals. From Ciudad Serdan, drive south toward the town of Esperanza for about 2.5 km (1.6 mi), to the first bridge. Turn right, drive under the bridge, and then get out of the stream bed by driving onto the road to the left. Over the next 2.5 km

The Sarcofago, El Pico de Orizaba (Rich Weber photo)

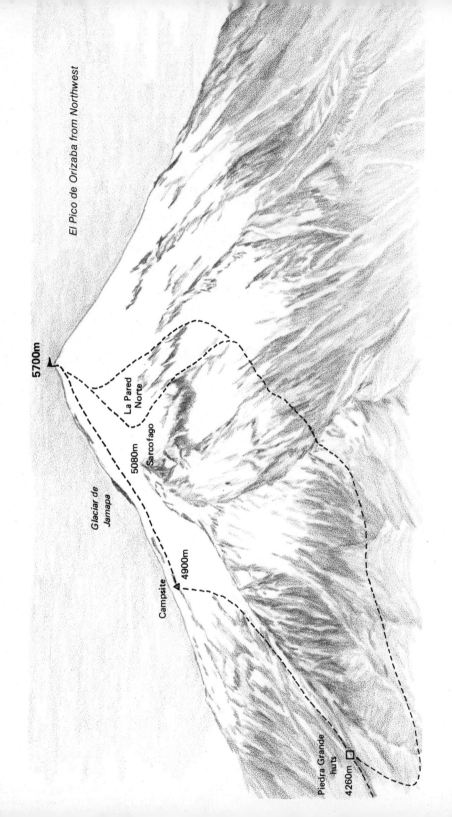

El Pico de Orizaba from Northwest

5700m

La Pared Norte

Glaciar de Jamapa

5080m

Sarcofago

Campsite

4900m

Piedra Grande huts

4260m

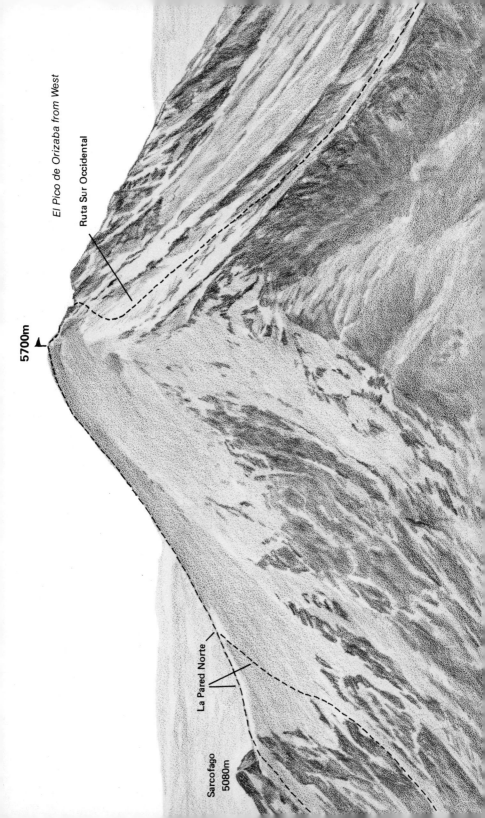

El Pico de Orizaba from West

Ruta Sur Occidental

5700m

La Pared Norte

Sarcofago
5080m

(1.6 mi), you pass through two villages. At the second village the road turns east, headed just north of Sierra Negra; the road is much more rough from this point on. From here five hours of hiking brings you to the Cueva del Muerto, at 3900 m (12,800′). Of the two choices, I prefer the approach that leads directly from Ciudad Serdan; the disadvantage of hiking a slightly longer distance is out-weighed by the ease of locating a safe place to leave the automobile, and renting pack animals, should this be desired. If the climb is made late in the season, water will be scarce; and the use of animals will become attractive.

As you pass beneath Sierra Negra, a small pass can be seen ahead, bounded by a rocky ridge to the left. The cave is on the far side of the ridge, less than a kilometer north of the pass. It is situated beneath overhanging rocks on a long shelf about 10 m (33′) wide. The Cueva del Muerto is on the left flank of a wide grassy valley, which offers attractive campsites for those who do not wish to use the alternative form of shelter offered by the cave.

Hike up the valley for 2 km (1.2 mi), and cross the lower, eastern ridge. It is not necessary to head for the saddle between the Torrecillas and Orizaba; continue traversing to the left. A gully descends from Orizaba, bounded by two small rocky buttresses; the gully may or may not be filled with snow. Climb this gully, or the rocks on each side of it, until two rock bands are reached beneath the crater rim. Skirt the rock band on the left, and the actual summit is 10 m (33′) higher and 100 m (328′) beyond the point where the crater rim is first reached. The summit is six to nine hours from Cueva del Muerto.

One cannot help but notice two prominent peaks southwest of El Pico de Orizaba, Las Torrecillas and Sierra Negra. Las Torrecillas, at 4700 m (15,420′), is a fine scramble, and Sierra Negra (4400 m; 14,436′) is a class 2 ascent from the northeast. Less scree will be found on the western and southern slopes of Sierra Negra than on the other sides.

Of the three high volcanoes, El Pico de Orizaba is the highest and most remote. In contrast to Popo and Ixta, Orizaba is not surrounded by sprawling urban areas, and it offers limitless possibilities for backpacking and trekking on its lower slopes. The mountain is surrounded by several Indian villages; many are reachable only by trail. Visiting such a village could be the highlight of a trip to Mexico. If you should happen to visit such a village, please don't act like the obnoxious tourist on the Reforma, or play anthropologist. Try not to attract too much attention, although a *gringo* walking into such a village with a brightly colored backpack is sure to attract some interest. In many cases, the inhabitants will show a great deal of hospitality, but don't count on obtaining food or lodging. Civilization is already creeping into the most remote of these villages, and it is only a matter of time before the consumer society takes over the subsistence society. I have just received a circular from a travel agency advertising such a journey to a village on the eastern slope of Citlaltepetl.

On Glaciar de Jamapa, El Pico de Orizaba (Rich Weber photo)

[Above] *Approaching the summit of Orizaba, Glaciar de Jamapa*
[Below] *Rocks of the crater rim, El Pico de Orizaba (Rich Weber photos)*

[Above] *The summit of El Pico de Orizaba*
[Below] *The return to Piedra Grande, El Pico de Orizaba (Rich Weber photos)*

Nevado de Toluca (Rich Weber photo)

CHAPTER FIVE

OTHER VOLCANOES

There are several other mountains worth visiting in Mexico. Often these other mountains are utilized as "training climbs" for the three highest volcanoes, but they are worthwhile objectives for themselves. All of the mountains are over 4260 m (14,000′), and the list below spans the width of the country. The easternmost and westernmost peaks, Cofre de Perote and Nevado de Colima, respectively, are less than 100 km (62 mi) from the Gulf of Mexico or the Pacific Ocean. None of these mountains has any permanent snow, but seasonal snow may be present, especially in the late fall and early winter.

COFRE DE PEROTE (4282 m; 14,048′)

Cofre de Perote is 50 km (31 mi) north of El Pico de Orizaba, and 30 km (18.6 mi) west of the city of Jalapa. Approach as for El Pico de Orizaba (see map on p. 83) is by driving north on Highway 140 from the town of Acatzingo. From El Seco, drive another 95 km (59 mi) to the town of Perote, an interesting place with a colonial fortress worth visiting. There are two dirt roads that lead southeast from Perote, serving the numerous microwave towers that surround tho peak The preferable road is the northern one; it is not as steep and is in a little better condition than the southern road. Drive as far as the vehicle and road permit. Nine kilometers (5.6 mi) from Perote, a trail branches to the south. Hike up this trail, amid scores of aerials, cables, and other reminders of the electronic age. After about 5 km (3.1 mi), the trail ends at some metal cabins, located at the western false summit. Hike northeast to the summit rocks, which are climbed by means of a class 3 chimney on the southwest side.

By continuing east on Highway 140, one can visit the charming city of Jalapa.

Cofre de Perote

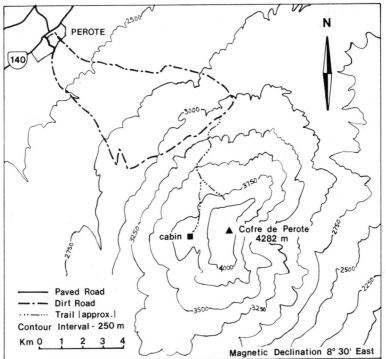

LA MALINCHE (4461 m; 14,436′)

Before Cortés landed at Veracruz, his soldiers defeated a Mayan war party. The spoils of that victory included 20 young females. Among them was a beautiful and intelligent woman, whom the Indians called Malintzin, a title of honor meaning "rain." The Spaniards mispronounced her name as Malinche, and she became Cortés' wife, aide, and interpreter. Legends have surrounded Malinche, the most popular being La Llorana ("Weeping Woman"). With long white robes and floor length hair, her ghost is seen at night, crying in agony over the actions that resulted in the betrayal of her race 400 years ago.

La Malinche has become a popular day hike in recent years as a conditioning climb for the higher volcanoes. It is 20 km (12.4 mi) northeast of Puebla, but most ascents begin in the town of Huamantla, on the northeast side of the mountain (see map on p. 83). From Puebla, drive north on Highway 119, past the city of Tlaxcala to Apizaco. Those driving from Mexico City get off Highway 190-D near San Martin Texmelucan and take Highway 117 to Apizaco. From Apizaco, take Highway 136 east to Huamantla. On the west-

La Malinche

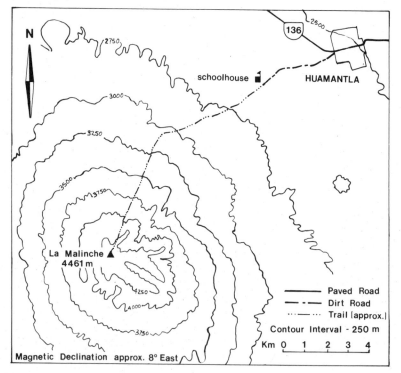

Market day (Rich Weber photo)

ern side of Huamantla, there is a PEMEX station across the street from a store and a restaurant. Head south on a road from here, and after a short drive you'll reach a school and a small playground. Park the car here. Don't leave anything of value in the automobiles at the schoolhouse; numerous thefts have been reported. Hike through the forest up to treeline. Whenever a fork is encountered, take the one leading toward the mountain. Above the trees, the route is obvious and leads up grassy slopes to the high point. The hike should take six hours from the schoolhouse. It can be done in a day from Puebla by getting an early start. Occasionally, snow hinders progress on the higher slopes.

NEVADO DE TOLUCA (4704 m; 15,433′)

This is Mexico's fourth highest mountain, and it is unique in that one can drive into the crater of this extinct volcano. The Aztec name for this mountain is Xinantecatl ("The Naked Man"). Nevado de Toluca has two summits, the higher named Pico del Fraile ("Friar's Peak") at 4707 m (15,433′) to the south, and Pico de la Aguila ("Eagle's Peak") at 4620 m (15,157′) on the northern side of the crater rim.

Take Highway 15 headed west from Mexico City toward the city of Toluca. Before reaching Toluca, take a bypass—Paseo Tollocan—leading south around the city. At the southern edge of Toluca, turn left (south) onto Highway 130, the main road leading into Toluca from the south. After some distance, Highway 130 turns right, leading to Temascaltepec. Eighteen km (11.2 mi) farther, a road branches off to the left toward Sultepec. Follow this road for 7 km (4.3 mi) to a gravel road leading up the peak. Turn left off the highway, and after several switchbacks, the road circles around the north

105

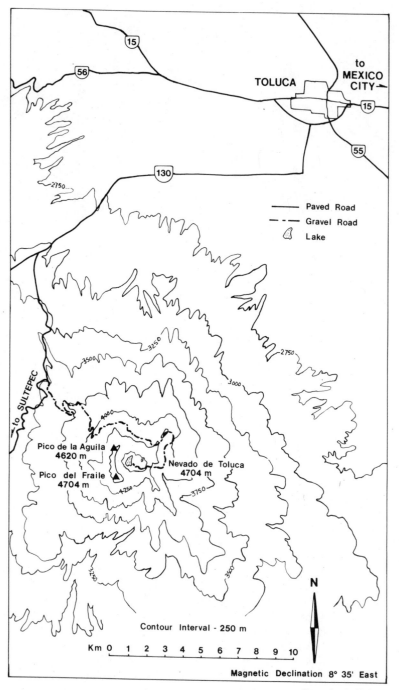

15

56

TOLUCA

to MEXICO CITY →

15

55

130

2750

— Paved Road
—·— Gravel Road
Lake

2750

3250

3500

3000

4000

to SULTEPEC

Pico de la Aguila
4620 m

Pico del Fraile
4704 m

4250

Nevado de Toluca
4704 m

3750

3250

3500

N

Contour Interval - 250 m

Km 0 1 2 3 4 5 6 7 8 9 10

Magnetic Declination 8° 35' East

Nevado de Toluca

Nevado de Colima

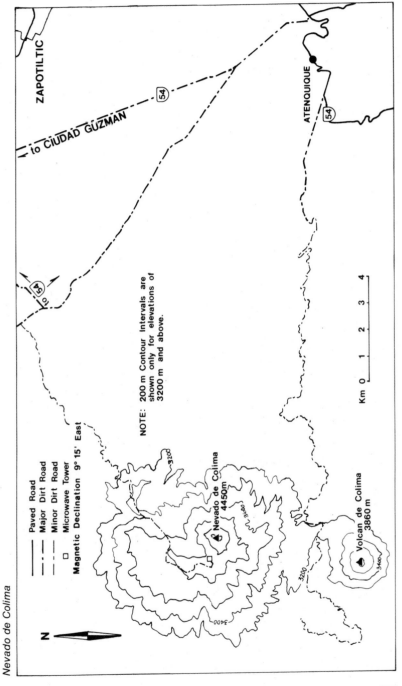

N

Paved Road
Major Dirt Road
Minor Dirt Road
□ Microwave Tower
Magnetic Declination 9° 15' East

NOTE: 200 m Contour Intervals are shown only for elevations of 3200 m and above.

Km 0 1 2 3 4

ZAPOTILTIC

to CIUDAD GUZMAN

54

45

ATENQUIQUE

54

3200

3400

3400

3200

3460

Nevado de Colima
4450m

Volcan de Colima
3860 m

side of the mountain to the east and eventually to the two lakes in the crater. There is a lodge located on the northern side of the mountain. It is similar in construction to the older lodge at Tlamacas on Popo.

The road ends at 4200 m (13,780'). Pico del Fraile is 500 m (1600') above the cars. The preferred routes of ascent are along the rims of the crater; the rock is much more sound on the ridges than on the faces beneath them. If there is a great deal of snow and ice, axes, crampons, and perhaps a rope should be carried.

In Toluca, market day is on Friday, and this is one of the largest and most colorful markets in the country. In spite of the attention given to it by tour groups, it is certainly worth visiting.

NEVADO DE COLIMA (4450 m; 14,600')

It is regrettable that Mexico's highest mountains aren't located in the central western section of the country. For those who enjoy the outdoors, the states of Michoacan and Jalisco contain some of the most beautiful mountains, lakes, and ocean beaches of the country. Most American hikers and climbers concentrate on the high peaks in the central part of the country; the mountains and valleys to the west are far more deserving of attention.

Actually, there are two mountains in the Colima massif. The southern and lower of the two peaks is Volcan de Colima, reportedly a still active volcano at 3860 m (12,655'). The northern peak is Nevado de Colima, an extinct volcano. The two mountains are near Ciudad Guzman in the state of Jalisco. Ciudad Guzman, is approximately 140 km (87 mi) south of Guadalajara, via Highways 80 and 54. From Ciudad Guzman, drive south on Highway 54 for 12 km (1.2 mi) and take a gravel road to the right. This road points directly to the mountain. After 8 km (5 mi) the road curves southeast toward the village of Atenquique; a fork goes in the opposite direction. Take the fork leading north, and after a kilometer (.6 mi), turn left onto a questionable dirt road. The road looks as if it will end immediately, but those with perseverance and an automobile in reasonable condition can travel a considerable distance. The road is about 20 km (12.4 mi) long and involves negotiating several switchbacks before crossing a pass at 3800 m (12,467'). After crossing the pass, the road turns left (south) and traverses the west slope of a smaller summit northwest of the true summit. The road ends at a microwave station at 4000 m (13,124'), separated from the main summit by a saddle. From here the true summit of Nevado de Colima is a scramble by any number of routes.

Volcan de Colima, the volcanic crater to the south, is reached by means of a dirt road headed west from Atenquique. You can easily reach this village by driving south from Cuidad Guzman on Highway 54; this section of the highway is not in the greatest condition. From Atenquique, drive up the road as far as possible. The road is approximately 25 km (15.5 mi) long and may be impassable in wet weather. Once above the trees, you can hike up the pumice slopes to the crater.

Glaciar de Jamapa, El Pico de Orizaba (Rich Weber photo)

Appendix A

RECOMMENDED READING

Backpacking in Mexico and Central America, by Hilary and George Bradt, Bradt Enterprises, 409 Beacon Street, Boston, Massachusetts 02115. In spite of the limited coverage given to Mexico, this book provides interesting, informative reading for those planning to visit the northern part of Latin America.

Terry's Guide to Mexico, edited by James Norman, Doubleday and Company, Inc., New York. Highly recommended. No traveler to Mexico should be without it. For the size of the area covered, it is surprisingly detailed and accurate.

The People's Guide to Mexico, by Carl Franz, John Muir Publications, P.O. Box 613, Santa Fe, New Mexico 87501. This is the definitive book that describes Mexico. All types of travelers will find it useful.

The Volcanoes from Puebla, by Kenneth Gangemi, Marion Boyars Publishers, Inc., 99 Main Street, Salem, New Hampshire 03079. This book is about the volcanoes from Puebla as much as *The New Yorker* is about New York. It is informative, poetic, humorous, and highly recommended for those who are tired of reading guidebooks to Mexico.

Appendix B

SPEAKING SPANISH

PRONUNCIATION GUIDE

h is never pronounced. *Helar* ("to freeze") is pronounced *ay-LAR*.
j is pronounced like the English *h*. *La Joya* ("the jewel") is pronounced *la HO-ya*.
ll is usually pronounced like the English *y*. *Llano* ("plain") is pronounced *YA-no*.
y is pronounced like the *y* in *yet*, never as the *y* in *only*. *La Joya* is pronounced *la HO-ya*.
ñ is similar to the *ny* in *canyon*. *La cañada* ("the ravine") is pronounced *la can-YA-da*.
que is pronounced as *kay*.

Abanico (ah-ban-EE-ko)
Acatzingo (a-ca-SEEN-go)
agua purificado (ah-gwa poo-ree-fee-KAH-do)
Agujas (ah-GOO-has)
Amacuilecatl (ah-ma-coo-WE-la-catl)
Amecameca (am-AY-ka-may-ka)
Antigua Flor (an-TEE-gwa flor)
Apizaco (ah-PEES-a-co)
Arista de Luz (ah-REES-tah day loos)
Arista del Sol (ah-REES-tah del sole)
Atenquique (ah-ten-KEE-kay)
Augusto Pellet (ow-GUS-toe PAY-yay)
Ayoloco (AY-oh-lo-co)
Balderas (bal-dair-AS)
Barriga (ba-REE-ga)
Cabellera (kah-bel-YAY-rah)
Cabeza (ka-BAY-sa)
Cañada Nahualac (can-YAY-da nah-WAL-ak)
carreterras (kar-ray-TAY-ras)
cartas topograficas (CAR-tas toe-po-gra-FEE-kas)
Chalchoapan (chal-cho-A-pan)
Chalco (CHAL-co)
Cholula (cho-LU-la)
Circuito Interior (sir-CWEE-to in-tay-ree-ORE)
Citlaltepetl (see-tlal-TAP-etl)
Cofre de Perote (KO-fray day pair-o-TAY)
Coscomatepec (cos-CO-ma-tep-ec)
Cruces (KROO-says)
Cruz Roja (kroos RO-ha)
Cuello (KWAY-yo)
Cueva del Muerto (ka-WAY-va del moo-AIR-to)
Ejercitio de Oriente (ay-hair-SEE-thyo day oh-ree-EN-tay)
ferreteria (fay-ray-tay-REE-ah)
Filo (FEE-lo)

garrafon (ga-rah-FON)
gasolina (gas-oh-LEE-na)
Glaciar de Jamapa (gla-see-AR day ha-MA-pa)
Glaciar Norte (gla-see-AR NOR-tay)
Glaciar Oriental (gla-see-AR o-ree-en-TAL)
Grietas (gree-AY-tas)
Grupo Alta Montaña (GROO-po AL-ta mon-TAN-ya)
Guerrero (gair-RAIR-o)
Huamantla (hua-MAN-tla)
huaraches (hua-RAH-chays)
Inescalables de la Cabellera (in-es-KA-la-blays day la ka-bay-YAIR-ahs)
Iztaccihuatl (ees-tay-SEE-watl)
Joya (HO-ya)
libre (LEE-bray)
llano (YA-no)
Malinche (mal-in-CHAY)
Nexcoalanco (nay-co-a-LAN-co)
Oreja (o-RAY-ha)
Oreja Derecha (o-RAY-ha day-RAY-cha)
Oreja Izquierda (o-RAY-ha ees-kee-AIR-da)
petroleo (pay-TRO-lay-o)
Pared Norte (pa-RED NOR-tay)
Pecho (PAY-cho)
Pico de Orizaba (PEE-ko day oh-REE-sah-ba)
Pico del Aguila (PEE-ko del AH-gee-la)
Pico del Fraile (PEE-ko del FRA-ee-lay)
Pico Mayor (PEE-ko ma-YOR)
Piedra Grande (pee-AY-dra GRAN-day)
Pies (pee-AYS)
Popocatepetl (po-po-ka-tap-ETL)
Portillo (por-TEE-yo)
Pueblo Nuevo (PWAY-blo NWAY-vo)
Querétano (kay-air-AY-ta-no)
Rodillas (ro-DEE-yas)
Ruta del Sol (ROO-ta del sole)
Ruta Sur Occidental (ROO-ta sur ok-see-den-TAL)
San Martín Texmelucan (san mar-TEEN tay-mel-OO-khan)
Sarcofago (sar-CO-fah-go)
Seguro Social (say-GOO-ro so-see-AL)
Sultepec (sul-TAP-ek)
supermercados (soo-PAIR-mair-KAH-dos)
Tenochtitlan (tay-noch-tay-TLAN)
Teopixcalco (tay-oh-PEEX-cal-co)
Texcalco (tay-CAL-co)
Teyotl (tay-OTL)
Tlalmanalco (tay-mahn-AL-co)
Tlachichuca (tal-chi-CHOO-ka)
Tlamacas (tal-MAWK-as)
Tlaxcala (tlax-CAH-la)
Torrecillas (tor-ray-SEE-yas)
Ventorrillo (ven-tor-REE-yo)
Zoapan (SO-a-pan)

CLIMBING VOCABULARY

the abyss	*el abismo*	ah-BEES-mo
the alpinist	*el alpinista*	al-pe-NEES-ta (masculine)
	la alpinista	al-pe-NEES-ta (feminine)
the arête	*la arista*	ah REES-ta
to arrive	*llegar*	yay-GAR
(at the summit)	*(a la cumbre)*	(a la KOOM-bray)
the ascent	*la subida*	soo-BEE-da
the avalanche	*el alud*	ah-LOOD
	la avalancha	ah-va-LAN-cha
the belay	*el amarrado*	ah-ma-RAH-do
	el asegurado	ah-say-goo-RAH-do
to belay	*amarrar (to anchor)*	ah-ma-RAR
	asegurar (to secure)	ah-say-goo-RAR
the bergschrund	*la rimaya*	reem-AY-ah
the bivouac	*la vivaque*	vee-VAH-kay
the blizzard	*la ventisca*	ven-TEES-kah
the boots	*las botas*	BO-tahs
the buttress	*el contrafuerte*	kon-trah-fu-AIR-tay
the cairn	*la pirca*	peer-KAH
the (high) camp	*el campamento (alto)*	kam-pa-MEN-to (AL-to)
the candle	*la bujía*	boo-HEE-ah
	la vela	VAY-la
the carabiners	*los mosquetones*	mos-KAY-tone-ays
the chimney	*la chimenea*	chee-may-NAY-a
the climb	*la subida*	soo-BEE-dah
to climb	*subir*	soo-BEER
the climber	*el escalador*	es-ka-LA-dor (masculine)
	la escaladora	es-ka-LA-dor-a (feminine)
the climbing instructor, master	*el profesor de alpinismo*	pro-fay-SOR day al-pe-NEES-mo (masculine)
	la profesora de alpinismo	pro-fay-SOR-a day al-pe-NEES-mo (feminine)
the cloud	*la nube*	NOO-bay
the col	*el cuello*	KWAY-yo
the compass	*el ámbito*	AM-bee-to
the cornice	*la cornisa*	kor-NEE-sa
the crampons	*los grampones*	gram-PON-ays
the crevasse	*la grieta*	gree-AY-ta
danger	*peligro*	pay-LEE-gro
the descent	*la bajada*	ba-HA-da
east	*este, oriente*	ES-tay, o-RYEN-tay
exposed	*expuesto*	eks-poo-ES-to

the flashlight	*la antorcha*	an-TOR-cha
	electrica	ay-LEK-tree-ka
	la linterna	leen-TAIR-na
flat	*llano*	YA-no
the fog	*la niebla*	nee-ABE-la
the food,	*los comestibles*	ko-mays-TEE-blays
i.e. provisions		
to freeze	*helar*	ay-LAR
frozen	*congelado*	kon-hay-LAD-o
the (white)	*la gasolina*	gas-ol-EEN-a
gasoline	*(blanca)*	(BLAN-ka)
the glacier	*el glaciar*	gla-SEE-ar
the gloves	*los guantes*	GWAN-tays
the guide	*el guía*	GEE-ah
the hammer	*el martillo*	mar-TEE-yo
height	*altura*	al-TOO-ra
the helmet	*el casco*	KAS-ko
help!	*¡socorro!*	so-KO-ro
high	*alto*	AL-to
the hut	*el refugio*	ray-FOO-he-o
	el albergue	al-BER-gay
the ice	*el hielo*	e-AY-lo
the ice axe	*el piolet*	pee-o-LAY
the ice field	*el banco de helado*	BAN-co day ay-LA-do
the ice hammer	*el martillo de hielo*	mar-TEE-yo day e-AY-lo
the ice piton	*la clavija de hielo*	kla-VEE-ha day e-AY-lo
icy	*helado*	ay-LA-do
the (down) jacket	*la chaqueta (de plumón)*	cha-KAY-ta
		(day ploo-MON)
to jump	*saltar*	sal-TAR
the kerosene	*el petróleo*	pay-TRO-lay-o
the (pocket) knife	*el cuchillo*	koo-CHEE-yo
	(de bolsillo)	(day bol-SEE-yo)
the map	*el mapa*	MA-pa
the matches	*los fósforos*	FOS-fo-ros
the moraine	*la morrena*	mor-RAY-na
the (high) mountains	*las montañas (altas)*	mon-TAN-yas (AL-tas)
the mountaineer	*el montañero*	mon-taw-NAY-ro
		(masculine)
	la montañera	mon-taw-NAY-ra
		(feminine)
the mountaineering	*el equipo*	ay-KEE-po day
equipment	*de alpinismo*	al-pe-NEES-mo
the mule driver	*el arriero*	ar-re-AY-ro
north	*norte*	NOR-tay
the pack	*la mochila*	mo-CHEE-la
the pack animals	*las acémilas*	ah-SAY-mee-las
the peak	*el pico*	PEE-ko
	el picacho	pee-KA-cho
the pitons	*las clavijas*	kla-VEE-has

the plateau	*el altiplano*	al-tee-PLA-no
the porter	*el portador*	por-ta-DOR
the precipice	*el precipicio*	pray-see-PEE-see-o
the rappel	*el rappel*	rap-PEL
the ravine	*la cañada*	kan-YA-da
	la garganta	gar-GAN-ta
to rent, charter	*fletar*	flay-TAR
the ridge	*la sierra*	see-AIR-a
the road	*el camino*	ka-MEE-no
the rock	*la piedra*	pee-AY-dra
	la roca	RO-ka
the rockfall	*la caída*	ka-EE-da day
	de piedra	pee-AY-dra
the loose	*el terreno suelto*	tay-RAY-no SWEL-to
(solid) rocks	*(sólido)*	(SO-lee-do)
the rope	*la soga*	SO-ga
	la cuerda	KWAIR-da
the route	*la ruta*	ROO-ta
the scree	*el aluvion*	ah-loo-ve-ON
the snowbridge	*el puente de nieve*	PWEN-tay day nee-AY-vay
the (new) snow	*la nieve (reciente)*	nee-AY-vay
		(ray-see-EN-tay)
the (powder) snow	*la nieve (polvorosa)*	nee-AY-vay
		(pol-vo-ROS-a)
the snow drift	*la ventisca*	ven-TEES-ka
south	*sud, sur*	sood, soor
steep	*escarpado*	es-kar-PA-do
stop!	*¡alto!*	AL-to
the stove	*la estufa*	es-TOO-fa
the stream	*la corriente*	ko-ree-EN-tay
the summit	*la cumbre*	KOOM-bray
	la cima	SEE-ma
the sunglasses	*las gafas oscuras*	GA-fas OS-koo-ras
the sweater	*el suéter*	SWAY-tair
the talus	*el talud*	ta-LOOD
the tent	*la tienda*	tee-EN-da
the trail	*la huella*	oo-EL-yah
to traverse	*atravesar*	ah-tra-vay-SAR
the valley	*el valle*	VA-yay
the village	*el pueblo*	PWAY-blo
the water	*el agua*	AH-gwa
the water bottle	*la botella de agua*	bo-TAY-ya day AH-gwa
west	*oeste, occidente*	o-WES-tay,
		ok-see-DEN-tay
the wind	*el viento*	vee-EN-to
the windbreaker	*el rompeviento*	rom-PAY-vee-EN-to
to zigzag up	*subir en zigzag*	soo-BEER en zigzag

CLIMBING PHRASES

Is there a guide in the village?	*¿Hay algún guía en el pueblo?*
We would like to climb the mountain tomorrow.	*Quisiéramos subir la montaña mañana.*
Crampons are essential.	*Son esenciales grampones.*
Will I need a rope and an ice axe?	*¿Voy a necesitar una cuerda y un piolet?*
The climb is very steep.	*La subida es muy escarpada.*
You will need ice pitons when climbing the face.	*Necesitará usted clavijas de hielo para subir por la pared.*
Beware of the crevasses.	*Cuidado con las grietas.*
We will have to spend the night in a mountain hut.	*Tendremos que pasar la noche en algún refugio.*
We might lose our way in the blizzard.	*Pudiéramos extraviarnos en la ventisca.*
Do you like mountaineering?	*¿Le gusta el alpinismo?*
You will become snow-blind if you don't use your goggles.	*Le va a cegar el reflejo de la nieve, si no pone las gafas oscuras.*
Can you let me have some cream for sunburn?	*¿Me puede dejar la crema contra la quemadura de sol?*
Did you have an easy climb yesterday?	*¿Tuvo usted una subida fácil ayer?*
We reached the summit at noon.	*Llegamos a la cumbre al mediodía.*
What mountains are there in this region?	*¿Qué montañas hay en esta región?*
Can we rent pack animals here?	*¿Podemos faltar aquí las acémilas?*
Have you done any climbing?	*¿Ha escalalado usted antes?*
The new snow is not good for climbing.	*La nieve reciente no es buena para subir.*
I must adjust my crampon bindings.	*Tengo que ajustarme las ataduras de los grampones.*
I don't like the snow; it is dangerous.	*No me gusta la nieve; es peligrosa.*
The snow has frozen overnight.	*La nieve se ha helado durante la noche.*
There has been an accident on the mountain.	*Ha habido un accidente en la montaña.*
Send for a doctor.	*Mande buscar un médico.*

Send for the mountain rescue team.	*Mande buscar el equipo de salvamiento.*
What is the matter with you?	*¿Qué le ocurre?*
I don't feel well.	*No me encuentro bien.*
I feel very ill.	*Me siento muy mal.*
I am nauseated.	*Me dan náuseas.*
I feel weak.	*Me siento débil.*
He (she) is suffering from pneumonia (pulmonary edema).	*Él (ella) está enfermo de pulmonía (edema pulmonar).*
He (she) must be taken to a hospital.	*Hay que llevarlo (la) a algún hospital.*
Is your digestion all right?	*¿Está su digestion bien?*
He (she) has broken his (her) arm.	*Él (ella) se ha roto el brazo.*
He (she) has fractured his (her) skull.	*Él (ella) se ha fracturado el cráneo.*
You have had a bad concussion.	*Ha tenido una conmoción seria.*
I am injured.	*Estoy herido.*
Have you sprained your ankle?	*¿Se ha torcido un tobillo?*
He (she) is snow-blind.	*Él (ella) está ciego del reflejo de la nieve.*
Your foot is frostbitten.	*Su pie esta tumido.*
The injured climbers were brought down on stretchers.	*Bajaron en camillas a los alpinistas heridos.*
They lost their way and a rescue party set out to find them.	*Se extraviaron y un equipo de socorro salió a buscarlos.*
A mountaineer was injured (died) in a fall.	*Un alpinista se hirió (murió) en una caida.*
We will need a stretcher.	*Necesitamos una camilla.*
He (she) cannot walk.	*Él (ella) no puede caminar.*
Please help us!	*¡Por favor, ayúdenos!*
We need help.	*Necesitamos ayuda.*

Appendix C
EQUIPMENT LIST

What follows is a list of the equipment that I carry when visiting the volcanoes. Others may wish to add more items, and some may be able to do without an altimeter and candles.

Clothing
wool socks (three pair)
long underwear
wool trousers with belt
wind pants
light cotton shirt
two sweaters
wind breaker
scarf
down jacket
wool cap
sun hat
dark glasses (two pair)
mittens (two pair)
waterproof cagoule
gaiters

Climbing gear
mountaineering boots
ice axe
crampons
swami belt
carabiners
runners
prusik slings
120' - ⅜" rope

Other
camera (with red and yellow filters for black and white film)
Spanish-English dictionary
road maps
guidebooks

Camping Equipment
frame pack
knapsack
first aid kit
sun cream
lip cream
two one-liter water bottles
compass
altimeter
first aid kit
toilet kit
toilet paper
plastic tarp (for emergency shelter)
sleeping bag
foam pad
spoon, bowl, cup
headlamp
candles
matches
kerosene stove
fuel container
cooking pots
dishwashing material
water jug
water purification tablets

Appendix D

METRIC CONVERSIONS

Meters to Feet

5700 m = 18,701'
5600 m = 18,373'
5500 m = 18,045'
5400 m = 17,717'
5300 m = 17,389'
5200 m = 17,061'
5100 m = 16,733'
5000 m = 16,405'
4900 m = 16,076'
4800 m = 15,748'
4700 m = 15,420'
4600 m = 15,092'
4500 m = 14,764'
4400 m = 14,436'
4300 m = 14,108'
4200 m = 13,780'
4100 m = 13,452'
4000 m = 13,124'
3900 m = 12,795'
3800 m = 12,467'
3700 m = 12,139'
3600 m = 11,811'
3500 m = 11,483'
3400 m = 11,155'
3300 m = 10,827'
3200 m = 10,500'
3100 m = 10,171'
3000 m = 9843'
2900 m = 9515'
2800 m = 9187'
2700 m = 8858'
2600 m = 8530'
2500 m = 8202'
2400 m = 7874'
2300 m = 7546'
2200 m = 7218'
2100 m = 6890'
2000 m = 6562'

Feet to Meters

18,750' = 5715 m
18,500' = 5639 m
18,250' = 5562 m
18,000' = 5486 m
17,750' = 5410 m
17,500' = 5333 m
17,250' = 5257 m
17,000' = 5181 m
16,750' = 5105 m
16,500' = 5029 m
16,250' = 4952 m
16,000' = 4876 m
15,750' = 4800 m
15,500' = 4724 m
15,250' = 4648 m
15,000' = 4571 m
14,750' = 4495 m
14,500' = 4419 m
14,250' = 4343 m
14,000' = 4267 m
13,750' = 4191 m
13,500' = 4115 m
13,250' = 4039 m
13,000' = 3962 m

12,750' = 3886 m
12,500' = 3810 m
12,250' = 3734 m
12,000' = 3657 m
11,750' = 3581 m
11,500' = 3505 m
11,250' = 3429 m
11,000' = 3352 m
10,750' = 3276 m
10,500' = 3200 m
10,250' = 3124 m
10,000' = 3047 m
9750' = 2971 m
9500' = 2895 m
9250' = 2819 m
9000' = 2743 m
8750' = 2666 m
8500' = 2590 m
8250' = 2514 m
8000' = 2438 m
7750' = 2362 m
7500' = 2285 m
7250' = 2210 m
7000' = 2133 m

INDEX

Abanico del Ventorrillo (Popo), 56
Acatzingo, 82
accidents, 34-35
acclimation, 33-34
Agujas, Las (Ixta), 76
altitude, problems of, 33-35
Amacuilecatl, La (Ixta), 22
Amecameca, 43
Antigua Flor, La, 84
Arista de Luz, La (Ixta), 75-76
Arista del Sol, La (Ixta), 72-74
Augusto Pellet hut (Orizaba), 86
Ayoloco, Glaciar de (Ixta), 19, 20, 74
Ayoloco hut (Ixta), 74
Aztecs, 8, 11-14

bandits, 36-37
Barranca del Cobre, 7
Bonpland, Aime, 18

Cabellera, La (Ixta), 22, 76
Cabeza, La (Ixta), 75-76
Camacho, Luis, 22
car rental, 28
Careaga, Alfredo, 23
Carlos V, 14
cerebral edema, 34
Chalchoapan (Ixta), 75-76
Cholula, 44
Ciudad Guzman, 108
Ciudad Serdan, 82-84
climate, 37-38
Club Citlaltepetl, 35
Club de Exploraciones de Mexico, A.C.
  (CEMAC), 8, 20, 35
clubs, mountaineering, 35
Cofre de Perote, 103
Colima, Nevado de, 7, 105
Colima, Volcan de, 105
Cordillera de Anahuac, 7
Cordillera Neovolcanica, 7
Cortés, Hernando, 14-18
Cruces, Las (Popo), 48-52
Cruz Roja, 34, 35
Cuello, El (Ixta), 75-76
Cueva del Muerto (Orizaba), 97

Daignon, Alexander, 18

Diaz, Bernal, 16
Diaz, Pedro, 23
Dios y Montana, 35
Directa al Pecho (Ixta), 75
dogs, 40
driving precautions, 28-29

Echeverria, Luis, 23
Eduardo San Vincente Route (Ixta), 76
equipment, 25-27
Esparza, Adolfo, 22
Esperanza Lopez Mateos hut (Ixta), 74

fauna, 24
Fearn, Walker, 19
fire, 39
flora, 24
food, 29-30

geology, 24
Glaciares Orientales hut, 76
Gomara, Lopez, 16-17
Grietas, Las (Popo), 52
Grupo Alta Montana Route (Ixta), 76
Grupo de los Cien, El, 35
Guadalajara, 108
guerrillas, 37
guides, mountain, 35-36

health, 32-35
Hernando Manzanos Route (Ixta), 76
history, 11-23
Hotel Fausto, 84
human impact, 39-40
Humboldt, Alexander von, 18, 19

Iglú hut (Ixta), 74
illness, 32-35
Inescalables de la Cabellera, Las (Ixta),
  76
Iztaccihuatl, 7, 19-20, 22
  first ascent, 19-20
  climbing routes, 72-76
  approaches, 42-43, 66-72

Jalapa, 103
Jamapa, Glaciar de (Orizaba), 88

kerosene, 26

Larios, Juan de, 18
litter, 8, 86

McAllister, Otis, 20-22, 23
Malinche, La, 104-105
Mangas, Roberto, 22
maps, 27-28
markets, 8, 37, 105
Mexican War, 18-19
Mexico City, how to get out of, 40-41
Montano, Francisco, 17-18
mountain sickness, 33

Nexcoalanco, 66-72, 75
Nieto, Juan Gabriel, 23
Norte, Glaciar (Popo), 52

Octavio Alvarez hut (Orizaba), 86
Ordaz, Diego, 14-19
Oreja Derecha, La (Ixta), 76
Oreja Izquierda, La (Ixta), 76
Oriental, Glaciar (Orizaba), 88
Otis McAllister Route (Ixta), 76

pack animals, 36
Pared Norte, La (Orizaba), 93
Paso de Cortes, 43-44
Pecho (Ixta), 66
Peimbert, Juan, 22
Perote, 103
pharmacies, 32, 34
Pico de la Aguila (Nevado de Toluca),
   105
Pico de Orizaba, El, 7, 8, 18-19, 22,
   first ascent, 18-19
   climbing routes, 88-97
   approaches, 82-88
Pico del Frail (Nevado de Toluca), 105
Piedra Grande huts (Orizaba), 84-93
Pies, Los (Ixta), 72
police, 37
Popocatepetl, 7,
   first ascent, 14-18
   climbing routes, 48-56
   approaches, 42-44
Portillo (Ixta), 72-74
Puebla, 13, 19, 42, 44
pulmonary edema, 33

Queretano hut (Popo), 56
Quetzalcoatl, 12

Republica de Chile hut (Ixta), 74

rescue, 34
Reyes, Señor, 84
Reynolds, Lt. William F., 19
roads, 8, 28-29
Rodillas, Glaciar de las (Ixta), 74
Ruta del Sol, La (Ixta), 76
Ruta Sur Occidental (Orizaba), 93-97

Salis, James de, 20
San Rafael, 43
San Vincente, Eduardo, 76
Scott, Maj. Gen. Winfield, 18
Seco, El, 82-83
Seguro Social, El, 34
Sierra Madre Occidental, 7
Sierra Madre Oriental, 7
Sierra Negra, 97
Sierra Volcanica Transversal, 7
skiing, 26-27
snow conditions, 37-38
Socorro Alpino de Mexico, 34, 35
Sonneschmit, 19
Spanish, 110-116
stoves and fuel, 26

Tenochtitlán, 11-12
tents, 26
Teopixcalco hut (Popo), 56
Texcalco hut (Popo), 52
Teyotl hut (Ixta), 76
Thurmer, Rigo, 84
Tlachichuca, 84
Tlamacas, 44, 48, 52
Toluca, 105
Toluca, Nevado de, 105
Torrecillas, Las (Orizaba), 22, 97
trains, 28
transportation, 28-29
   car rental, 28
   bus, 28
   trains, 28

Valvovinos, Issac, 22
Ventorrillo (Popo), 22, 52-56
Veracruz, 19, 40
Vincente Guerrero Lodge, 44

water, 8, 32
weather, 37-38
Whitehouse, H. Remsen, 20

Zedwitz, Baron von, 20